THE
DEVIL IN
CONNECTICUT

Gerald Brittle

BANTAM BOOKS
TORONTO · NEW YORK · LONDON · SYDNEY

THE DEVIL IN CONNECTICUT
A Bantam Book / November 1983

ISBN 0-553-23714-4

Published simultaneously in the United States and Canada

Bantam Books are published by Bantam Books, Inc. Its
trademark, consisting of the words "Bantam Books" and
the portrayal of a rooster, is Registered in U.S. Patent and
Trademark Office and in other countries. Marca Registrada.
Bantam Books, Inc., 666 Fifth Avenue, New York, New
York 10103.

To S.T.J.

Introduction

In February 1981, a young man by the name of Arne Cheyenne Johnson was arrested in Connecticut and charged with murder. Under ordinary circumstances, such a crime would have been given brief mention in the local press, and the matter would then have quickly faded from public view. But there was something different about this case, and within a month the story became front-page news around the world. Attention was focused on this particular murder because the young man claimed—in an unprecedented legal defense—that he was not guilty of the crime by virtue of diabolical possession.

What the press did not know at the time, because the essential facts were still cloaked in secrecy, was that the murder actually represented the culmination of a horrendous religious case that had begun fully eight months before, in the town of Brookfield, Connecticut.

This book is a reconstruction of the entire Brookfield possession case, from its disturbing origin to its tragic end. Places, persons, dates, and events that are mentioned can be substantiated in the public record. The specific research data, which comprises the bulk of this text, was taken directly from the victims of the event; from the Warrens, who were the chief investigators of the case; and from photographs and tape-recordings made on the scene while preternatural phenomena were in progress. Beyond being an extraordinary attack on a typical American family by violent spirits of darkness, what ultimately makes this case unique and sets it apart from the rest is that the siege was orchestrated not by some random demonic force, but by a devil of a very high order. The result was pure iniquity. This will stand as one of the worst cases of possession to occur in the twentieth century.

G.D.B.
February 1983.

Possession belongs to a class of extraordinary facts which only happen by the special permission of God. . . . It is a rough imitation, a sort of infernal parody on the incarnation of the Word, permitted by Providence, in order to show what would one day become of man if he preferred the service of the prince of darkness to that of the King of Heaven.

—*The Devil*
  Paris, 1871

Chapter I

The white church steeple rising high above the lush green hillside denotes from afar the quaint, historical town of Brookfield, Connecticut.

The soaring spire belongs, appropriately, to the local Congregational Church, which has stood on that site since the town's Puritan elders settled in the area more than two centuries ago.

Brookfield is truly as old as America itself. It has witnessed every epoch in American history; its sons have fought in every war from the Revolution to Vietnam.

Colonists began inhabiting the region seventy-five years before the Declaration of Independence was even written. Farming was the principal occupation at that time, yet of no less vital concern to the early settlers was religion—fire-and-brimstone religion.

The original Puritan Congregationalists who settled in the area took the Bible as the unchallenged master plan for salvation and the indisputable guide for the behavior of mankind. Stocks and whipping posts were constructed for those penitents who did not get the "message." It is no surprise that Brookfield one day became a battleground for good and evil.

Indeed, the very origin of the community was religious in nature. By 1755, the congregation had grown sufficiently large to declare itself independent, and the district came to be known as Newbury Parish.

Two years later, in September 1757, a meetinghouse was dedicated on the site of what is now the Brookfield Congregational Church. That autumn day was doubly special, as the building not only was dedicated, but the first order of business within it was the ordination of a young seminary student by the name of Thomas Brooks. In 1788, Brookfield was named after him.

Thomas Brooks died the same year as George Washington, in 1799, but Brookfield prospered and grew. Along the "Turnpike," which ran through the center of town, were built stately homes, schools, churches, stables, and mills.

What began as Newbury Parish is now Brookfield Center. And at first glance, little appears to have changed over the centuries. The same white clapboard homes, picket fences, and stone hitching posts stand along the Turnpike of old, known today as Route 25. Lilacs and forsythia still abound in spring; autumn still continues to produce a blaze of color. In summer, the dominant sound echoing through the hillsides on warm Saturday afternoons is the tinkle of ice in a stiff gin and tonic. Life today is placid in Brookfield.

For one family living virtually within the shadow of the Congregational Church, however, the tranquility of life in Brookfield came to an abrupt, tragic end in the summer of 1980.

                              *   *   *
It is evening.

The date is July 1, 1980.

The mellow ring of the church bell tells the village it is now eight o'clock.

In the backyard of the Glatzels' house, the decision is made to go for one more truckload of dirt before knocking off work for the day.

A gentle breeze blows through the tall birches as the weathered red dumptruck is backed up to the base of a towering hill of dirt. A yellow derrick then proceeds to fill the load bed with great heaps of rich Connecticut topsoil.

"Take it away," the foreman says with authority.

Slowly, David Glatzel forces the heavily loaded dumptruck away from the hill, and, making the hard, straining sound of a diesel engine, transports the dark soil across from his left foot to his right.

"David," his mother calls from the back door, "come in, son. It's time to call it a day."

The little boy tilts the dumptruck and spills the load of dirt. "I'm coming, mommy," he answers.

Carl and Judy Glatzel live in a beige, extended one-story ranch house built twenty-five years ago. They moved there from Norwalk, Connecticut, in 1969. Less than a mile from Route 7—the famous antiqueing run— the Glatzels' house is situated on a hill, surrounded by an acre of wooded land. From the front of the house, the vista of sky, hills, and dramatic orange sunsets is enthralling.

Carl and Judy Glatzel have been married for twenty-seven years. They have four children. Carl Glatzel, age forty-six, is a big, rugged man with a burly gray beard. He looks like a cross between Commander

3

Schweppes and Kriss Kringle. Carl is a specialty mechanic on heavy-duty construction machinery and is responsible for maintenance of costly, complicated equipment. He works long, hard hours and sleeps like a log at night. Carl is a straightforward, honest man, and he has no tolerance for fantasy or laziness. His children adore him, but when he tells them to jump, they ask for permission to come down.

Judy Glatzel is an attractive blond with deep-set eyes, and she looks considerably younger than her forty-four years. Petite and frail in appearance, she is nevertheless a no-nonsense mother. Judy's life revolves around her home and family, and she enjoys being a homemaker. Though quiet, she is disarmingly perceptive, and will challenge a lie the moment it's uttered.

The Glatzels have a daughter and three sons. Debbie, age twenty-six, is their eldest; after her come the three boys: Carl, Jr., fourteen; Alan, thirteen; and David, eleven.

Debbie is tall and lean, with deep green eyes and long auburn hair pulled back into a ponytail. She has a precocious seven-year old son named Jason, the product of a brief marriage when she was a teen-ager. Though taller, Debbie looks very much like her mother.

The Glatzel boys are big, beefy kids who markedly resemble their father. Yet, each has his own distinct personality. Carl, Jr., loves motorbikes and weight lifting. Like most boys his age, he can't wait to get his driver's license.

Alan, on the other hand, is quiet and contemplative. He's an observer, with a penchant for photography and home computers. The family expects that Alan will pursue a white-collar career.

And then there is David—a roly-poly eleven-year-old. He is the family's teddybear. Unaffected, with a

4

sweet personality and a ready giggle, David prefers to be outside, rearranging the landscape with his fleet of toy trucks and earth-movers.

When David comes into the house, Judy directs him straight to the bathtub.

"I wanna watch 'Popeye' after my bath," David tells his brother in the living room.

On the couch, Alan is watching television. It is day 241 of the hostage crisis in Iran, and the show he is watching reports that an embassy officer, Richard Queen, may come home within the week.

Downstairs, in the workshop, Carl, Jr., is helping his father recondition one of their 340cc snowmobile engines. Snowmobiling is one of the family's favorite pastimes, and they own four machines.

Standing on a chair in front of the linen closet is Debbie Glatzel. On the floor beside her is a half-filled cardboard carton.

"Do you use these white muslin curtains anymore, mom?" she asks.

"You can take them," Judy answers.

Debbie passes them to her mother, who folds them and places them in the carton.

Debbie is packing; tomorrow she intends to begin a whole new life.

Later in the evening, after the boys have gone to bed, Carl and Judy Glatzel have a long, serious discussion with their daughter. Debbie has not lived at home for many years, but the step she is about to take is a major one. Her parents want to be sure the decision she has made is the right one.

Debbie Glatzel is a professional dog groomer at a kennel in nearby Newtown. However, she lives in Bridgeport, some twenty miles to the south, in the home of Mary Johnson. Mary, divorced, is struggling to raise three young girls and an eighteen-year-old son, Arne. Debbie has lived with Mary for more than four years. During that time, Arne and Debbie have fallen in love, and they plan to get married in the fall.

However, life in Bridgeport has become untenable for Debbie and the Johnsons. Not only is it difficult for Debbie to commute to work, but the city itself is tawdry and crime-ridden. Arne Johnson hates the city and wants out. He has long yearned for a better place to live—not just for himself, but for his mother and sisters. Fighting, drunkenness, and constant danger in the streets is not his way, and he's determined to leave it.

For six months, therefore, Arne and Debbie searched the newspapers for a large house on a wooded plot north of Bridgeport, in upper Fairfield County, where children and pets would be accepted. It seemed an impossible task, until one day late in April 1980 they found precisely what they were looking for in the *Bridgeport Post*.

The house, set back in the woods off a rambling country road, was just across the Brookfield line, in Newtown. The place was perfect. It had everything they wanted. Even George, their amiable sheepdog, was welcome.

"This is *your* house," the owner told Debbie with an odd intensity. "I *want* you to have it." The place would be vacant in July.

Renting the house was calculated to solve some complicated problems. Mary Johnson has had to raise her own three children, plus a nine-year old niece, without a husband or child support. Consequently, Arne Johnson, since the day he could walk, has been the man of the family. He is the cohesive force. He quit high school in the tenth grade to help support the family.

His sense of compassion and responsibility was evident even when he was a child, when he took his collected earnings as a paperboy, $250, and bought his mother an old car so she wouldn't have to walk almost three miles along the highway to her job as a cleaning woman at the Holiday Inn.

Now Mary Johnson, at the age of forty-two, is incurably ill with a painful form of colon cancer, further complicated by a thyroid problem. The objective is for both Arne and Debbie to work, pay the bills, and take the burden off Mrs. Johnson, who needs rest and care. Arne and Debbie have decided the main house will be for Mary and the girls, while they'll live together in the apartment in the attached extension to the house.

"Your plans sound good," Carl tells his daughter. "But you're talking about raising a son of your own, plus taking on the responsibility of three young girls, a mother-in-law who requires expensive medical attention, a large house, a full-time job, and a husband. That's a very tall order!"

"I know," admits Debbie. "But it's no different than the way we're living now, except Arne and I aren't married yet. It isn't going to cost us any more to move, and besides, there's no landscaping work for Arne in the city."

"All right, then let's talk about your finances. How much is it going to cost you to live there each month? And how much have you paid out so far?"

"The agreement is five hundred fifty dollars a month for the rent, which includes all utilities. We couldn't afford it if we had to pay extra for fuel, electricity, and whatnot," she says candidly.

"Did you get this in writing?"

7

"Mary was supposed to sign the lease today," Debbie tells him.

"How much of a deposit did you put down?" asks Judy.

"One month's rent," Debbie replies. "A total of eleven hundred dollars."

"Christ!" says Carl. "Where did you get that kind of money?"

"We chipped in," Debbie replies. "Arne and I used our own money to pay the deposit, and Mary used the money that would've gone for rent in Bridgeport this month."

"You spent everything you had, didn't you?" Judy asks.

"Yes," Debbie concedes reluctantly. "But Arne has a job. He starts as a tree surgeon next month. And until then, he's working part time with me at the kennels, and he's got private landscaping jobs, too."

"Why don't you wait a few months before taking on such a large burden," Judy suggested.

"We can't, mom. We've already paid the money, and Mary's already forfeited the Bridgeport house. Whether we like it or not, we have to move tomorrow."

"It sounds to me like you're cruising on luck right now," Carl concludes, reaching for his wallet. "And luck won't buy food." He counts out five twenties and hands them to Debbie. "I know you've all been working hard, but let this help in the meantime. You can pay it back when you get settled. But for now, I don't want to see you all step off on the wrong foot when you're trying to get ahead."

"Thank you, daddy," Debbie says with true appreciation. "I really do love you."

The talk is over.

Carl and Judy Glatzel get up and go to bed.

Debbie will sleep on the couch.

Unknown to all, they have just spent the last normal day of their lives.

Chapter II

Wednesday, July 2, 1980, began normally for Debbie Glatzel. She rose early and filled the trunk of her car with clothes and cartons. She then drove twenty miles south to Bridgeport to pick up Arne and Jason, her son, and their sheepdog, George. By ten-thirty all were traveling north on Route 25, heading for the house in Newtown.

The temperature was ninety degrees and climbing when they pulled into the driveway shortly before eleven that morning.

"Is this where we're gonna live now, mommy?" asked Jason, leaning enthusiastically over the backseat and gazing wide-eyed at the house.

"That's right," Debbie answered. "Do you like it?"

"Oh yeah, I do!" He jumped out of the car and ran up the long dirt driveway, followed by the playful sheepdog.

Debbie and Arne got out of the car just as eagerly.

Arne Johnson is a short, muscular young man with bushy blond hair and a quiet voice. Although he is only eighteen years old, there is strength to his face. Arne has not lived an easy life, and his character has been developed through perseverence. For Arne Johnson, things now seemed to be coming together.

Arne and Debbie stood taking in the whole scene. It was a ranch house, painted army green with beige shutters. The house was separated into two parts: to the right was the larger, main house, and on the left was an attached addition about the size of a one-car garage. Towering above the place stood stately oak and maple trees in full bloom. The sounds of birds echoed through the surrounding woods. Compared to the sirens and other discordant noises of city life in Bridgeport, the tranquility was utterly calming.

Before going inside, Arne and Debbie took a slow walk around the perimeter of the house. Disappointment began to tinge their enthusiasm. Grass was overgrown everywhere, and the backyard was a snarl of briar and brush. The reddish brown roof was weathered and would soon need repair. Paint was curling off the woodwork; the whole exterior was dry and desperately in need of fresh paint. The front door was weathered. Untrimmed yews stood on either side of the entrance steps, partially obscuring the front windows.

"It's worse than I thought," Arne admitted.

"Yea, it's pretty bad," agreed Debbie. "But we'll have the whole thing fixed up by the end of the month. Besides, there's nothing wrong with the inside."

Debbie then told her son, "Jason, we're going into the house now. Come on."

Arne opened the front door, and they stepped into a suffocatingly hot atmosphere that carried an unpleasant musty smell.

As Debbie began sliding open windows to air the place out, Arne walked back to the front door and, holding it open, called the dog. The dog romped up to the base of the front steps, then stopped.

"Come on, boy! Come on!" Arne commanded, but the gray and white sheepdog barked and backed away to the center of the lawn. Arne let the dog have his way, figuring somehow he knew the house was too hot inside.

Unlike the exterior, which distinctly required attention, the inside seemed all right.

"So far so good," Debbie reported to Arne. "Karen, the girl who lived here before, seems to have moved everything out."

"How come she moved?" asked Arne.

"Something about getting a divorce, I think. She moved back to Bridgeport with her daughter. The rent was too much for her alone."

At the far end of the hall, Arne opened the door of the right rear bedroom. Debbie and Jason came in a few steps behind, to discover a full-size, filled waterbed with a mirrored canopy occupying almost the entire bedroom.

"Oh boy!" Jason exclaimed, ready to plunge onto it.

Debbie grabbed him by the shoulder. "Forget it," she said. "It's not ours, and if you broke it we couldn't afford to replace it. Stay off!"

Though it was still hot in the house, Debbie felt a sudden, distinct chill in the hall just underneath the access door to the pull-down stairs to the attic.

"Well, what do you think?" Arne asked.

"I think we ought to unload the car and get the furniture set up," Debbie answered curtly.

"No, I mean about staying here—and paying high rent for this kind of place."

"Are you nuts? We're moving in. Today! Right now!"

"You don't have to yell, Debbie."

"Who's yelling?"

"You are, Deb."

"Get off my back, dammit!" she shot back.

"My name's not dammit, and I'm not on your back," Arne protested.

"You are too, dammit!" she yelled. "So cut the crap and let's move the hell in here!"

"What's wrong with you?"

"Nothing the hell's the matter with me! I'm fine! What the Goddamn hell's the Goddamn the matter with *you*?" she said viciously.

Debbie had never spoken like that before. Arne stared at her for a long moment, then walked out to the car.

Later, Debbie went outside and joined Arne as he was taking cardboard boxes from the car. Feeling terrible, she said, "I'm sorry for yelling. I didn't mean it, really. I don't know what came over me."

"There's such a thing as getting too mad, Debbie."

"Today's a whole new beginning, Arne. Please, forgive me for shouting at you. Sweetheart, you're not mad at me, are you?"

"No, I'm not mad," he said. "I don't think I *can* get mad at you; I love you."

For the next hour, Arne, Debbie, and Jason worked diligently. They unloaded the car, then brought up their furniture, which had been stored in the basement. Their belongings were sparse but sufficient.

A plywood enclosure took up almost a quarter of the cellar space, and looked to be an excellent storage area. But the enclosure was firmly locked, and Arne couldn't get it open. It was another annoyance, like the waterbed.

Upstairs, a different problem was developing. While Arne was rummaging around the basement, Debbie discovered that the keys Mrs. Johnson had given her wouldn't open the lock to the addition built onto the house. Peering through the curtain, she saw that the apartment—into which Arne and she were supposed to move—was still occupied. Debbie knew the owner's daughter had lived in the apartment, but she was to have vacated the premises by July 1.

After discussing the matter, Arne and Debbie decided to call Mrs. Johnson. On the phone, Debbie learned that when Mary Johnson had signed the lease, the owner had mentioned that her daughter, who was moving out West for health reasons, had changed her plans and would not be vacating the apartment until mid-July. Arne and Debbie were incredulous. Yet, considering the alternative of returning to the city, they determined to take the problem in stride.

It was twelve-thirty when they got back to the house. Debbie began unpacking boxes and filling dresser drawers, while Arne scoured the bathroom. Jason explored the woods outside.

Around one o'clock Debbie's mother arrived. Judy had not yet been to the house, and had promised to bring lunch and work with them through the afternoon. She had brought David, Alan, and young Carl with her.

After lunch, Debbie and Arne took Judy Glatzel on a tour of the house, then asked for her opinion.

"How come you didn't take that nice place over in Botsford?" was Judy's oblique reply. "It had everything: ponds, a barn, landscaped property, a modern house."

"It was right next door to a cemetery," Debbie replied. "Plus, one of the barns standing there was half

15

burned down. 'A burnt barn is a jinxed farm.' The place wasn't right. I liked it, but I couldn't live there."

"Well, Debbie, I'll be honest with you—this place isn't any better. I don't like it!" Judy said in no uncertain terms. "There's something creepy about it. It's not a happy home."

"Oh, mom, it'll grow on you. I know it's dark and needs some cheer, but give us a month and you'll see the difference."

Suddenly they were jolted by the sound of the heavy basement door slamming. The force was enough to make the windows rattle.

"Good God!" Debbie exclaimed, swinging the door open. "Get up here! *Right now!*"

Carl, Alan, and David Glatzel, heads bowed, climbed the cellar stairs like prisoners of war, captured on the battlefield of play.

Debbie sternly reminded them that they were there to work, not to play, and told them to ask Arne what had to be done.

To the young Glatzel boys, Arne Johnson was their big brother. They trusted him.

Accordingly, Arne assigned appropriate jobs to the boys. Carl was given a putty knife and told to free up the windows that were painted shut. Alan was issued a broom and instructed to sweep the floors. David was to check all closets and cupboards, and throw away any junk that didn't belong there.

The boys set off to perform their duties, little knowing that these would be the last minutes of an innocent childhood. For within the hour an incident would occur that would mark the beginning of an incomprehensible, diabolical seige that, in time, would forever change the lives of every member of the Johnson and Glatzel families.

16

All was calm for the better part of an hour, when suddenly the quiet was broken by the boys' giggling in a far room of the house. Inevitably, they had discovered the waterbed. The adults found Carl, Alan, and Jason rolling around on the waterbed, making "waves." David, predictably timid, was reluctant to engage in roughhouse, and stood watching from afar.

At a stern word from Judy, the boys reluctantly got off the bed and trooped out of the room, followed by the adults.

However, David, stayed in the room. Walking over to the foot of the bed, he noticed the surface was still slightly undulating. He then turned and gazed out the window and saw a light rain beginning to fall.

Suddenly, incredibly, David felt what seemed to be two large hands—like those of a man—pressing on his stomach. A moment later, David was shoved backward onto the waterbed. He landed flat on his back.

At five feet tall and weighing 150 pounds, David is a weighty child, and considerable force would be required to knock him over.

David quickly turned, expecting to see Jason or one of his brothers making a hasty retreat.

But that wasn't the case. When David Glatzel turned to see who had pushed him, his mouth dropped open.

Standing before the boy at the foot of the bed, bearing a wild, menacing look on its face, was a man, or at least the visage of a man. Suddenly, David realized he could see *through* the man!

The child was seized with terror. His body shook. As he watched, the specter slowly lifted its arm and pointed directly *at him*.

His heart pounding, his body shaking, his mind aswirl, David watched the figure back away and disappear from view. The boy shuddered with cold fear.

David moved off the bed slowly, never taking his eyes off the spot where the thing had appeared. He eased out of the room without shifting his gaze.

David's mind was reeling as he stood in the living room. He couldn't understand what had happened to him. All he could understand was that he was frightened, and the fright was real.

When Debbie called him and asked him to help his brother Alan carry a carton into the bedroom where the waterbed was, David gasped and shouted. "*No! No! I won't go back in there!*"

"What's the matter with you?" Debbie asked.

"Nothing," he said crossly, and walked past her into the kitchen where Judy was working. "I want to go home, mommy. I want to go home now!"

"In a little while, David," she said, without looking up from the sink she was scrubbing.

"I want to go *now!*" he insisted. "I don't want to stay here."

"David, I'm sorry, but no!"

Frightened and feeling totally alone, David ran outside and refused to come back in. He sat with the dog under the tree on the front lawn out of the sprinkling rain. Tears streamed down the little boy's face as he looked back at the dark, now forbidding house.

Meanwhile, another strange episode took place in the waterbed room. Carl and Alan had maneuvered the carton into the bedroom and slid it into a corner. When they went to leave, the door closed—by itself. No matter how they twisted and manipulated the doorknob, they could not get it to open the door. Something was not right. Feeling trapped, Alan and Carl began to yell for help. The sound of their voices should have carried through the empty house, but no one heard them.

When Alan tried to turn the doorknob once again, it functioned perfectly.

"Didn't you hear us calling?" Alan asked Debbie.

"No," she said. "Why?"

"We got locked in that bedroom."

"That's neat, Alan. You're real smart," she remarked wryly, and went into the kitchen, where her mother was still working.

"What's David's problem?" Judy asked.

"He's bored, I think. Or maybe the heat got to him," Debbie answered.

Judy accepted the explanation without comment.

"You know, I've been working in here most of the afternoon," Judy said, "and I've gotten things clean—or at least I've gotten the dirt off—but it all looks so dull. I was in the living room before, and I polished and repolished that long mirror on the wall until my arm ached. But there's a haze in it, deep inside; it won't give a true reflection. And when I walk into the back of the house, I get an odd feeling. Are you sure you want to go through with this?"

"I'm not sure about anything, mom. All I know is that this is better than Bridgeport, and we've already got a lot of money sunk into the rent. All we can do is try to make it work out."

At that moment, the owner's daughter knocked at the front door. Debbie let the young woman in.

"Hi, my name's Lois," she said. She was in her mid-twenties, with dark hair, a slender figure, and an attractive face.

Debbie introduced herself and her mother, and they all shook hands.

"What's with the little boy out there? Is he always like that?" Lois asked.

Judy and Debbie glanced out the window and saw David sitting against the tree, his back to the house.

"That's David, my brother," Debbie said. "He's not feeling very well today."

"Well, everything going okay?"

"No, not exactly," Debbie said. "To start with, I thought you were going to move out of the apartment next door on the first."

"No; sorry. I haven't gotten it together yet," Lois said. "Maybe around August."

"August! But we paid good money to rent this place—and we rented the *whole* place!"

"You'll have to take that up with my mother," Lois retorted.

"We're going to," Debbie said. "Next, there's a waterbed in the back bedroom. When's that gonna go? We can't set our furniture up in there until that thing's taken away."

"I think Karen said she was coming back for it tomorrow," Lois answered.

"Where are we supposed to sleep tonight?"

"Why don't you sleep on the waterbed?"

"I'm not sleeping on any other bed than my own. You tell that girl to get that damn thing out of the house by tomorrow, or I'll drag it out myself," Debbie declared. "And another thing—the cellar's a mess. Where's the key to unlock that storage room? We want to put some stuff in there."

"Oh, you can't use that room!" Lois exclaimed. "Nobody is to go in there!"

"Are you kidding? We're *paying* for this place, remember?"

"You rented it—you didn't buy it. Besides, I don't own the house. You'll have to talk to my mother about these things. I have to go now. Nice to meet you, Judy." The young woman then walked out the front door and returned to the attached apartment.

"This is ridiculous," Debbie said, on the verge of tears. "Today was supposed to be good, but everything's turning out wrong. And I'm not about to sleep on someone else's bed, especially an oversized air mattress full of stagnant water!"

After the owner's daughter had left, David walked up to the front door. "I want to go home," he insisted. "I don't want to stay here anymore. Can we go now?"

"This is too much!" Debbie exclaimed. "I can't work anymore. I can't even think. I'm going to tell Arne we're not sleeping here tonight." Then she told David to go wait in the car.

Having closed up the house, the last task was to bring the dog inside, and Arne literally had to carry him in. Dry dog food and a bowl of water were set out on the kitchen floor. Arne and Debbie expected to come back later in the evening to check on him, but the cellar door was left open just in case of accidents. Though they regretted having to leave him there, they knew he'd probably fall asleep soon.

Finally, the boys were rounded up, and the group returned to the Glatzels' home in Brookfield. It had been a difficult, fatiguing afternoon, hampered further by rain, and attitudes were dour. David was worst of all. He was cross and grumpy and spent the remainder of the day alone brooding in his bedroom.

At supper that night, although Arne and Debbie were still upset, it was David who was the real problem. Normally bubbly and giggling and full of life, he was now glum and long-faced and refused to talk. Efforts to cheer him up were met with, "Leave me alone," or, "I

21

don't have to answer you." Eventually, he just got up and walked away, leaving a plate full of food.

David Glatzel was carrying a problem that he felt no one would believe.

Later that night, however; after the other boys had gone to bed, he confided in his brother Alan.

Chapter III

"Alan? Are you asleep?"

"No. Why?"

"I'm afraid. Something happened to me today. I want to tell you, but you have to promise you're not gonna laugh. And turn on the light—the little one."

"Okay, I won't laugh." He turned on the light. "Now what?"

"Something happened to me today in that house, Alan."

"Me too. Me and Carl got locked in the bedroom with the waterbed. We couldn't get out. The doorknob wouldn't work. Then it would."

"Really?" David asked, relieved.

"Yeah! It was scary. What happened to you?"

"Something scary, too. In the same room! There was a man in there, Alan. But not a real man—a ghost man. He pushed me down on the waterbed!" David had raised his voice, then lowered it to a whisper.

"What did he look like?"

"He was an old man, and he was wearing regular clothes. But he looked crazy. And he pointed at me, Alan. And he *talked*, too! He was moving, like he was real. I mean, he *was* real, but he was moving, too."

"David, you're scaring me."

"Alan, I'm scared all over! That's why I'm telling you. I can't sleep. I keep thinking about it."

"You're not kidding me, are you? I mean, what you're telling me is pretty far out. If you were making this up, that would be . . . sick. You know?"

"I'm not lying! There's something in that house. I can see it from here!"

"What do you mean, you can see it from here? What do you see?"

"It's there with the dog." David put his hands up over his eyes as he continued, "George is running back and forth in the house. He's going crazy. He just ran down the cellar stairs, right now."

"You can see over inside the house, right now, sitting from here?"

"I can see it all, Alan."

"God. This is serious, David. Are you sure about this? I mean, are you sure you're sure?"

"Yep, I'm sure."

"Okay—you say the dog is over there flipping out. What about Arne and Debbie—and Mrs. Johnson and the girls? Tomorrow they're gonna move in there. This thing could go after them, too."

"I never thought of that," said David, reflecting on this new fear. "I gotta tell 'em," he reasoned out loud. "But how? You believe me, but they'll think I'm nuts."

"No, they won't," said Alan. "I won't let them. We'll just tell it to them the way it is."

David and Alan went into the kitchen. Arne and

Debbie were sitting at the table with Judy. Alan spoke first. "David wants to say something, and I think you better listen to him, because he's not kidding. Okay, David."

"Remember when you chased Jason and Carl and Alan out of the bedroom for being on the waterbed?"

"Right," they all said.

"Well, after they were gone, I stayed in the bedroom alone. I walked over to the window, and when I was standing there, I felt two hands push me on my stomach—like when someone pushes you in the pool. I didn't know what was happening. I didn't see nothin'—yet. Then he pushed me hard, and I fell back on the waterbed."

"Who? *Who* pushed you on the waterbed?" Judy asked, frowning.

"The old man. He was like a ghost, or something," David stated.

"David, is this a dream that you just had, and you woke up, and wanted to tell us about?" Arne asked.

"No. It's no dream. It didn't happen tonight. It happened this afternoon," answered David.

No one around the table knew what to say.

"Is that all that happened? I mean, is there more to it?" Debbie asked.

"Yeah. There's lots more," David said. "It's happening now."

"Okay, stop!" Arne directed. "This doesn't make any sense. Start from the beginning. You're telling us you saw a ghost in the house, in the waterbed room?"

"Right."

"How many times did you see it?"

"Once, then. But I see him now."

"You see him? Is it here?" Arne asked.

"No. It's at the waterbed house."

"What does it look like?"

"He had gray hair—no, white. And a small mustache—white. There was a mole up by his right eye."

"That's all you saw?" Judy asked. "Just a head?"

"No, I saw all of him," David revealed. "He was wearing a red plaid shirt. The sleeve on the left side was all torn apart and ragged. His pants were ripped, too. He had on old blue jeans, washed-out-like. There was a hole in the left knee of the pants. He scared me, like I told Alan, because he looked crazy, like he might try to hurt me."

"Was he solid or transparent?" Arne asked.

"What's that mean?," questioned David.

"See-through," his mother told him.

"I could see part of the room through him, but not a lot. He was mostly solid.

"When I first saw him," David continued, "he was just standing there, like he was letting me see him. I thought he was stiff. But then his arm, his left arm, began to move. He raised it up all the way and pointed his finger at me and stared."

"Then what?," said Judy.

"Then he talked to me. His finger was pointing straight at me, and he said—'Beware'!"

"Beware," Judy repeated with incredulity.

"This is too much," Debbie declared. "Is this some kind of joke, Alan? Because it isn't funny!"

"He's telling the truth," Alan said. "He's telling you more than he told me."

"What happened after that, David?" Arne asked.

"Nothing, really. He kind of just stepped back and faded away."

"Did he say anything else than 'Beware'?" Alan asked his brother.

"Nope. That's all he said—during the afternoon, at least."

"What does that mean?" Judy asked in a wavering voice. "Has this thing talked to you *again?*"

"Oh, yeah, mom, that's the rest of it," Alan announced. "David says he can see inside the house right now."

"I can do more than that," David said ominously.

"What are you talking about? What can you do?" Judy demanded.

"Calm down, mom," Alan cut in.

"Enough!" Arne said firmly. "I want to hear the rest of this. I want to know what's supposed to be going on there."

"I don't want to sit in here. I want to sit on the couch," David said, getting grumpy. Accordingly, all got up and moved into the living room.

"Okay?" Arne asked. "Now go on, David. When did it talk to you again? And what's this about George?"

"I didn't tell this part to Alan, because *he* told me not to tell anyone that he was there," David divulged. "He told me this before, just after I laid down in bed and closed my eyes."

"Who told you this—the old man?" Judy asked.

"He's not an old man anymore. He changed when the sun went down. Now he's different. I can't see him too clear. But now his body is all red, and his face is big and white, with black eyes. And coming out of his forehead he grew *horns.*"

"My God!" Judy said, struck with the impact of what David was saying.

Nervous, Debbie took out a cigarette and picked up the lighter on the coffeetable. When she flicked it, the flame roared all the way up to the ceiling. The incident was over in a second, but left all staring in wonder.

"It's here!" Alan exclaimed.

"No, it isn't," David replied calmly. "It's still at the waterbed house."

"David, he told you not to talk with us. Did he tell you anything else?" Arne asked.

"Yes," David said reluctantly. "He told me to . . . to take down the holy card of St. Michael in my bedroom. And he wants us to take all the crucifixes out of the house, too. He told me if I don't do these things, he's going to punish me."

"Oh, really," Judy mused. "Did you obey him?"

"No," David said. "I'm not gonna."

"What about George?" Alan asked his brother. "You were talking about him being scared before."

"How would you know that?" Arne asked. "And how would this thing be able to talk to you if he's not here?"

"Because I can't stop it, Arne," David told him honestly. "When I close my eyes, I can see inside the waterbed house just as if I'm there. The same thing happens if I put my hands up over my eyes."

Judy and Debbie didn't ask any more questions. They sat huddled together on the couch, their arms interlocked, aghast at what they were hearing. Arne retained his composure, though even Alan was beginning to get frightened.

"And if I asked you to put your hands up over your eyes, David, would you be able to see George now?"

"Yes," David replied. "But I don't want to. I don't want to see the ghost man."

"Okay," Arne said. "But can you tell me what you know about the dog?"

"He was in the basement before. He was scratching real hard at the door to that locked room downstairs. That's where the ghost man comes from. He was scratching it so hard that it made one of his paws bleed. The ghost man goes back and forth between the waterbed and the downstairs room. When George sees him, his eyes turn red and he runs in circles. He's scratched up the inside of the front door too. That's all I know."

"We're not moving into that house, Arne," Debbie said suddenly. "We're moving our stuff out of there first thing tomorrow. I'm calling your mother as soon as we get up in the morning and tell her not to move in. We should get our money back and start looking for another place."

While Debbie was talking, David was staring off into space. Then he said, "He—I mean the ghost man— just told me that you're not to tell Mary Johnson anything, ever! He doesn't want . . ."

"Stop!" Judy demanded. "What is this 'the ghost man told me' business?"

"I forgot to tell you," David said, caught off guard. "When he talks to me, I can hear him, even though I might not be seeing him."

"Oh, I'm sorry. I beg your pardon. I didn't understand," Judy said wryly. "Now it's taking over your mind!"

"No, it isn't," David replied. "I just hear him."

"What's this about my mother?" Arne cut in.

"The ghost man says that Mary Johnson is not to know he exists. Mary is his, he says. He's been 'interfering in her affairs' for a long time, and he says he's going to break her down; he wants her to do his work."

David's statement was mind-rocking, petrifying.

Debbie, her voice cracking, said, "If all this is true, then I'm not about to let Mary and those three little girls move into that . . . that house."

David replied immediately, "He wants to know if you're questioning him."

"He wants to know if I'm questioning him?" Debbie repeated sardonically. "I'm not about to answer that!"

"The ghost man just said that if you tell Mary Johnson anything whatsoever, you'll be sorry."

"Oh really?" Debbie said. "And what does the ghost man propose to do?"

Again, David's answer was immediate. "He says if you tell Mary he's there, you'll be blinded by midnight tomorrow."

"Lord," Judy mumbled.

"I don't know whether any of this is true," Debbie said. "In fact, I feel like I'm in the 'Twilight Zone.' But even if I am, I'm not going to let some kind of spiritual beast with horns in its head, that doesn't like crucifixes, and talks about blinding people, dictate what I can and can't do!"

"He's laughing at you," David said. "He says you'll see—tomorrow. He'll cause the waterbed to break by three o'clock tomorrow afternoon. He says, 'Bring a mop, bitch!' "

"David Michael Glatzel!" Judy cried.

At that moment, Arne Johnson began to shudder violently. "I just had this terrible, deathlike cold come over me," he said. "It's gone now, but for a few seconds I didn't have any warmth in my body."

"The ghost man did it," David declared. "He said it was to show you that he's in charge now. And if there's any more impertinence out of anyone, there's going to be unrelenting pandemonium in this house!"

"Impertinence?" Debbie said with amazement. "Unrelenting pandemonium?" David attended special reading classes at school, as he had a minor learning disability and vocabulary was not his strength. "Where did you get those words, David?"

"They're not mine, they're *his*," David answered. "I'm just telling you what he said to me."

"What does *impertinent* mean, David?" Debbie asked.

"I don't know," he replied.

"And what does *pandemonium* mean?"

"I don't know!" David said crossly, sensitive to his difficulty with vocabularly. "All I told you is what he told me."

"All right! That's it!" Judy said. "I don't want to hear any more about ghosts, the ghost man, nothing! David, Alan, go to bed. And I want you to sleep, not talk. Tomorrow this nonsense will be a thing of the past."

Chapter IV

Thursday, July 3, 1980, began in the Glatzel house with three important questions, directed at David.

"Do you remember what we were talking about last night, David?" Debbie asked.

"I remember," he said, "the ghost man."

"That's right, but was everything you told us last night true?"

"Everything," David said.

"And is that figure, that beast, still in the house today?"

"Yep! He's still there. He knows you're coming."

Arne Johnson was standing in the kitchen, listening. Debbie turned to him, and said, "I don't think we ought to move in there. These kind of things really do happen sometimes. And David's not lying. He doesn't know the first thing about this stuff. He won't even watch horror movies."

"Debbie, I don't think he's lying either. But I'm

not ready to throw the cards in yet. There's too much at stake. There's got to be some kind of rational explanation."

"Well then, name one," Debbie said.

"All right," said Arne. "David, I want to ask you a question, and I want you to be totally honest with me."

"I will, Arne," David said, "but I have been honest."

"Granted. But still answer my question—truthfully. Whatever you say, I won't tell on you. Now, there are drugs and pills that can make you say or even see the kind of things you've been talking about. So give it to me straight. Did you find some pill in the house yesterday and take it by accident?"

"No, Arne. I wouldn't take nothin'. Really. I told you what I did because it wouldn't have been fair not to. The ghost man even said that if I did tell you, he'd punish me. It was a favor."

"Okay, David, you're a good buddy. I believe you," Arne said. "I'm sorry if I maybe insulted you, but I had to check."

"Can I go outside now?"

"Yes, you can go outside, and thank you."

"Now what do you think?" Debbie asked.

"I dunno," Arne replied. "I never heard of such a thing."

"I'm going to call your mother," Debbie said. "Then let's go over to the house."

Debbie called Mrs. Johnson in Bridgeport, but there was no answer. Believing that Arne's mother must already have started out to the rental house, Arne and Debbie immediately drove over there.

When they arrived, though, Mrs. Johnson was not yet there. They walked up to the front door, expecting the sheepdog to start barking loudly. But there was no barking. They found the dog lying docilely on the living room floor. His fluffy coat was matted and dirty; saliva

34

had caked around his mouth; he had wet himself; and there was blood on his paw. The poor animal obviously had a traumatic night.

Arne approached the dog carefully, not sure how he might react. But George only licked Arne's hand. The right paw showed bleeding around the claws. Arne, feeling terrible, led George outside into the fresh air.

When Arne came back into the house, Debbie pointed to the inside of the front door. It was criss-crossed with scratch marks and there were spots of dried blood on the floor. David's portentous statements were beginning to ring true.

They checked the cellar and found scratch marks on the door of the so-called storage room, just as David had predicted. The dog had apparently tried to get into the room by pulling at the lower corner of the door.

"What do you think is in that room?" Arne asked.

"Come on, Arne, forget it," Debbie said. "Let's just go upstairs and get our stuff out of here. Yesterday my mother told me this wasn't a happy home, and she was right. David was right. Let's consider ourselves lucky that only the dog had to experience something."

Arne did not tell Debbie that while they had stood in the basement he had distinctly felt a finger tapping twice on his shoulder.

Upstairs in the living room, he said, "Let's go next door and talk with the owner's daughter, and then let's get hold of my mother, wherever she is. We've got to get our money back, or we can't do anything."

Precisely at that moment, Mary Johnson pulled into the driveway. Her three young girls sat in the front with her; the backseat and trunk were filled with boxes and suitcases. The girls were cheery and so was Mary. They had long been looking forward to the day. Arne and Debbie didn't spring the news on Mary immediately. First, they questioned her about the rental agreement.

"You already signed the lease, and gave the landlady all the money, right?"

"Right," Mary said.

"Do you have the receipt?" Arne asked.

Mary fumbled in her pocketbook and handed him a receipt for the rent. "She wouldn't give me a receipt for the security," she remarked. "And there was something else, too. It said in the paper that the rent included the utilities, but the other day the owner told me that the utilities were extra, not part of the rent."

For the next fifteen minutes, Arne and Debbie detailed the reasons why they should not rent the house. They explained about the unvacated apartment; they noted that the cost of utilities would drive up the monthly expenses by another two hundred dollars; and finally they told her what had happened to David. They urged her to reconsider, and together they would seek a return of the rent.

Arne and Debbie expected that Mary would understand. Unfortunately, she didn't.

"I just can't believe the two of you are doing this to me," Mary said. "I don't swallow that story about David: I think it's a lie. Maybe you've changed your minds about this house, but I haven't. I'm moving in. Besides, now I have no other place to go. I've put all my money into this place. If you don't want to live here, then don't. But we're moving in!"

Arne and Debbie were dumbfounded. Neither had ever seen Mary so stubborn.

"I want the keys to the house," she demanded. "If you two are going to walk out on me, then go ahead."

They were divided. Neither side would back down. Accordingly, twenty-four hours after they'd arrived at the house to start a new life, Arne and Debbie began to move out instead. They filled Debbie's car with as much as would fit, but it was apparent that they'd have to get a truck to carry the rest of their possessions. While they were working, the owner's daughter, Lois, came home, and Debbie confronted her.

Debbie claimed they had been cheated. Further, Debbie announced to the young woman that she wouldn't live in the place because it was haunted.

"That's ridiculous," Lois said.

"Is it?" Debbie shot back. "Yesterday my brother was sitting under that tree because he was scared silly after seeing the ghost of an old man in the bedroom where that waterbed still is."

"Your brother needs to see a psychiatrist," Lois replied.

"There's nothing wrong with my brother! He saw an old man with white hair and a mustache in that bedroom. It had a mole by its eye, and was wearing a red plaid shirt and dungarees. It also talks dirty and doesn't like crosses."

"Oh, that's just my grandfather," Lois said. "He's harmless. He's been around here for years. There's nothing to be afraid of with him."

"Well, I think I'll just take my chances in a normal house that doesn't happen to already be haunted."

"This is some kind of prank, so you can break a perfectly good legal agreement," Lois said. Then she left abruptly.

Debbie went back into the house and found Arne arguing with his mother. The house seemed to breed animosity. Unable to get through to anyone, Arne and Debbie took the dog and drove back to Brookfield.

It was noon when they arrived at the Glatzel house, where the central air-conditioning was a welcome relief. When David came in for lunch, Arne asked him casually, "How's it going?"

"I'm doing okay," the child replied, "but you're not. The ghost man is really mad at you, and says you're gonna get it because you told Mary Johnson about him."

"I don't want to hear it!" said Debbie. "Tell the ghost man to go to hell."

"This thing—this beast, as you called it—is very real to him," Judy said. "What do you think we ought to do?"

"Humor him, ignore him—who cares?" Debbie said in frustration. "We just went through a lot of grief to end the problem."

After lunch, Debbie called Patricia Giddings, her best friend and next-door neighbor. Debbie had noticed Pat's brother's truck in the driveway and knew he was visiting. He agreed to help Debbie and Arne move their belongings out of the rental house and arranged to meet them there in an hour.

Arne and Debbie then drove back to the house to try to reason with Mary Johnson again. But it was futile. She was not about to relinquish the first good thing that had come her way in a long, long time.

Mary Johnson's entire life has been a travail. At the age of fourteen she walked out of a difficult family situation and entered an Episcopal convent to become a nun. Four years later, on the day she was to take her vows, Mary declined: "I couldn't become a nun. I wanted a family."

In 1961, healthy and strapping, she married, and in January 1962 she bore a son, Arne Cheyenne Johnson. His middle name was derived from a television show, in the hope that he would exhibit the quiet strength of the show's star. Arne was born with bronchial pneumonia, and was baptized in the hospital, as everyone expected that he would die. But Arne survived.

A divorce and remarriage followed, and Arne's two sisters—Wanda and Janice—were born. Wanda also faced death at birth, the victim of an acute asthmatic condition. Janice was born with cerebral palsy. It took many years for "Janny" to overcome the disability, but with Arne's constant help and encouragement, she took her first steps into her brother's arms.

Amidst these difficulties, Mary's second husband left her. Yet, in 1971, Mary Johnson took on the responsibility of raising another girl, a niece. The infant's name was also Mary, and Mrs. Johnson raised little Mary with the other children as her own. In 1972, Mary Johnson contracted colon cancer, and then a near fatal thyroid condition.

Still, Mrs. Johnson endured. A strict and proper mother, she raised the children as Baptists. Church and Sunday school were mandatory for her son and daughters. Arne sang solos in the choir of Kings Highway Baptist Church, and his family listened proudly. To them, Arne was the man of the house.

In late 1976, Mary Johnson took in a boarder, Deborah Glatzel, to help pay the rent. Over the years, Debbie helped ease the financial burden in the home and became part of the family. Arne Johnson grew to love this girl who extended herself to all of them.

Now, as Arne and Debbie stood in the living room of the rental house that represented so much to Mary, they were caught in a crossfire of emotions. They were completely unable to communicate with the woman.

Hostility filled the air as Arne and Debbie silently collected the last of their belongings. Whatever doubts they may have had about their decision were allayed with the arrival of Karen, the young woman who previously lived in the house and had come to dismantle her waterbed.

"Did anything unusual ever happen to you while you were living here?" Debbie asked her.

"No, not really," Karen replied, unconvincingly.

"I think you're lying," Debbie said bluntly. "I asked you the question because your answer matters. This room, this room right here, is trouble, isn't it?"

"Yeah, you hit it right on the mark," Karen answered, sitting down on the waterbed. "I've had strange things happen to me here. Sometimes when I'm lying in bed, in the dark, a voice will fill the whole room, saying *Kaaarennn*. It gives me the creeps."

"What else?" Debbie asked.

"Chickens! I distinctly hear chickens clucking just outside the house at night—in fact, only at night—but no one around here owns chickens. I checked. Upstairs in the attic, sometimes I hear footsteps; and I always get goosebumps underneath the swing-down door to the attic, out there in the hallway.

"Lights seem to work on their own," she continued, "and doors open and close by themselves—open and then slam shut—even when I'm here alone."

"There's more to it," Debbie said. "There's actually a spirit in this house, isn't there? There's the spirit of a man here—with white hair and a white mustache."

The girl snickered. "That's not what showed itself to me. If there's a spirit, it's an evil one. From what I've been able to learn, it seems that some kind of witchcraft was once conducted here. And I think there's a profane altar in the locked storage room downstairs."

"What makes you think there's something evil here?" Debbie asked.

"I don't think, I know! When it happens, it always happens at exactly three o'clock in the morning," the young woman said. "Even if I'm sound asleep, it'll somehow wake me up a few minutes beforehand.

"First," she revealed, "I'll either hear my name called out from a distance—Kaaren—or I'll hear the sound of heavy breathing in the room with me. It's scary. You just *know* there's someone, or something, out there.

"And you sit there—and wait. Things get so still. Then it happens. The thing in the room gets into the bed with me! I mean, some kind of cold, damp body will actually get into this waterbed with me right here; something physical, with enough weight to force the bed down and cause movement. Oh no!" she cried suddenly.

Water was trickling out from under the frame of the bed into a pool on the floor. When Karen got up, her jeans were soaked. The screwdriver she'd carried in her back pocket had pierced the waterbed.

Debbie looked at her watch. It was two forty-five.

Shortly thereafter, Pat Giddings and her brother pulled into the driveway. With four people working, including Pat and her brother, it took only twenty minutes to load the truck.

Before leaving, Arne and Debbie went into the house and tried one last time. "Mary, it's not too late. In another twenty minutes we can empty the whole house completely."

But Mary wouldn't hear of it.

Debbie tried again. "Just go into the back bedroom and speak with Karen. Please! There's trouble in this house—she's experienced it."

"I don't believe you. I don't believe any of it," were Mary Johnson's parting words. "All I've got to

41

say is that if you leave this house today—don't come back!"

Arne started to reply, then gave up. "Let's go, Debbie," he said.

The split was complete.

Chapter V

Arne and Debbie felt a combination of guilt and relief about deciding not to stay in the rental house in Newtown. They were worried about Mary and the girls, but felt strongly that they were right in their decision. In time, they thought, Arne's mother would see the truth too.

When Arne and Debbie arrived back at the Glatzel house, they found Judy sitting alone at the kitchen table. Debbie immediately knew something was wrong.

"Young Carl has been picking on everyone today," Judy told her. "All afternoon he's been yelling and arguing—not just at me, but at Alan and Jason, and especially David. He's really been giving it to poor David, telling him he's crazy, and calling him names like 'Dracula' and 'fairy brain' and jumping out yelling boo! to scare him."

"Carl is doing that?" Debbie asked, amazed.

Judy nodded. "I don't know what's come over him.

Arne, you're going to have to talk with him. Carl listens to you, and I can't get through to him.

"But it's David I'm really worried about," Judy added. "He says this thing keeps talking to him. While you were gone, he told me how it had worked Mary Johnson into a tizzy about the house, and how she was furious and arguing with you. He also explained in detail how Debbie had talked with someone named Karen about a spirit in the waterbed room, and that she'd punctured the waterbed with a screwdriver. Are all those things true?"

"Yes," Debbie said, amazed. "What else has David said?"

"Let's see," Judy said, starting to count off items with her fingers. "It's going to *stab* David for telling us about him; it's going to 'retaliate' against you for letting Mary Johnson know he exists; it's going to 'invade' this house and bring hell down on this family; tomorrow David's hand will be burned in Norwalk; and, oh yes, it'll rain as we leave the picnic tomorrow afternoon. Anything else you need to know?"

Suddenly David cracked the bedroom door and walked into the kitchen. His face was drawn and pale, and his eyes were wide with terror.

"He's coming, mommy! He just left! He's coming to get me!"

"Who's coming, David?" Judy asked.

"He's coming to take me!" David cried. "You gotta stop him!"

"Who, David? Who?"

"Him! That thing—that figure from Mary's house. It's coming now!" he cried frantically. "It's coming down Route Twenty-five! It's floating fast above the treetops!"

David began trembling, as Judy rose to her feet beside him.

44

"It just went past the Brookfield Center Post Office! It's getting closer!"

Terror had overtaken the boy. Tears welled up in David's eyes while his voice rose until he was screaming.

"He's by the church! Oh no! He's above Silvermine Road! He's coming fast! Stop him, mommy! He's coming for me! He's almost here! Help me, mommy!" David pleaded wildly.

"My God! What'll I do?" Judy cried. "Holy water! I've got holy water! I'll get the holy water against it!" She ran into her bedroom and grabbed a small bottle of holy water from atop her dresser.

"He's coming! He's crossing the Giddings' yard," David reported hysterically.

Then, his eyes wide open, his mouth agape, David backed away from the door as far as he could get.

"It's here!

"It's on the back porch!

"It's . . . it's at the back door!"

Three ominous knocks suddenly sounded.

Arne and Debbie blanched, while Judy threw a spray of holy water on the back door, declaring, "In the name of the Father, the Son, and the Holy Ghost—leave us in peace!"

Staring at the kitchen door, David reported with momentary relief, "It . . . it worked. He hates it. He's moved into the backyard."

All seemed well for a few seconds.

"Oh no!" David cried. "Now he's coming around the front. He's gonna try and get in the front door!"

Judy ran to the front door, blessed it, with the sign of the cross, and commanded, "In the name of Jesus Christ, go back to where you came from!"

"That stopped him again," said David, more confident now.

45

"Is it gone?" Judy asked desperately.

"No. He's moving around the house looking for another place to get in," David said.

The entity then attempted entry through every door, window, and access point—including the cellar and fireplace. Frantically, Judy threw holy water wherever and whenever David told her to. She felt both silly and scared, casting around holy water and commanding unseen spirits to leave, but she also believed her son.

Finally, David reported that the entity had stopped trying to get in and was now sitting on a lawn chair in the backyard. Sure enough, a lawn chair that had been folded-up on the porch had mysteriously been set up on the lawn.

Soon David told them the spirit was leaving. First it went next door to the Giddings house, where it inspected Arne and Debbie's belongings in the basement, then it "drifted back above the treetops" to the rental house in Newtown.

The weird experience left everyone shaken and disturbed. They all wanted to declare the episode ridiculous and forget about it. But their fear was real. Suppose the thing came back? Suppose it got in when someone was home alone?

Fortunately, that afternoon, the incident proved to be an isolated one. Apprehension diminished by evening, but the larger problem of the house in Newtown still had to be faced. When Carl Glatzel returned home from work, Arne and Debbie knew they would have to give some reason for their presence in the house. No one had yet told him about the so-called spirit problem.

Knowing her father didn't believe in such things, Debbie held nothing back as she described the events that had persuaded them to not take the rental house.

"You let five hundred dollars go down the drain

because an eleven-year-old boy told you there might be a ghost in that house?" Carl Glatzel was incredulous.

"That's right," Debbie said, "along with the statements of two other women who lived on the property, the dog's unusual behavior, and all the craziness that's gone on here in this house since the whole thing began."

"What do you have to say, David?" Carl asked.

"She's telling the truth," he replied.

David might as well have said nothing. Carl simply looked at him and said, "I don't buy it. You're all dreaming."

"See! Even daddy thinks you're crazy," Carl, Jr., said hostilely. "Mom, Debbie, Arne, Alan, Jason, and David are all flipping out. They're all nuts. They've gone cuckoo!"

The discussion soon degenerated into a shouting match that broke up the meal. Young Carl, usually reserved and quiet, put on quite a vitriolic display that no one could believe. But matters soon calmed down, and talk turned to the July 4th picnic.

At eleven o'clock it was time for bed, and it was decided that Jason would sleep with Alan and David in their room. Arne and Debbie would spend the next few nights in the sleeping bags on the living room floor. At eleven-fifteen, when the three boys were settled, Debbie went into the bedroom to check on Jason and say good night.

"Give mommy a kiss, and then the lights are going off," Debbie said. Jason sat up in bed and reached out to embrace her.

Suddenly, Debbie shrieked in agony, and, with her hand over one eye, backed away in excruciating pain.

It was a freak accident. As Jason had reached out to his mother, his fingernail had gone straight into her eye.

47

The pain was devastating. She felt like her eye had been gouged out.

Debbie was rushed to the emergency room of New Milford Hospital and treated for a scratched cornea. The doctor applied tranquilizing eyedrops, taped a bandage over the eye; and gave her the address of an eye doctor to consult the next morning. Depressed by all that had gone wrong that day, Debbie began to cry out of the one good eye she had on the way home.

When Debbie awakened the morning of July 4, 1980, she couldn't see. She'd lost muscle control in the good eye as well. Remembering the sinister prediction a few nights before, she wondered if she was doomed to darkness for trying to warn Mary Johnson about the entity. Debbie prayed silently as Arne and Judy took her to the eye specialist.

An hour later, Debbie's vision was restored. Her prayers were answered.

When they returned from the doctor, David was playing in the backyard. "Are you okay, Debbie?" he asked with concern.

"Yes. I can see fine." Though she didn't want to pursue the matter, she felt the question had to be asked: "David, do you know how this happened to my eye?"

"No," he said truthfully. "I didn't see it. But the ghost man was laughing real hard when it happened, and he said he did it."

"Ghost man, hell," Debbie said disgustedly, "this thing isn't a ghost, it's a Goddamn beast!"

" 'The beast,' it just said to me," David corrected.

"Where is the thing now?" Judy asked.

David turned around and pointed. "He's standing on the hill watching us. He's been watching me all morning. He's trying to find a way to get into the house."

"This is ridiculous," Judy said. "We've got to put a stop to this nonsense."

"But how?" Debbie asked. No one had an answer.

That afternoon, the family drove to Norwalk for a July 4th picnic with relatives on the shore. For a few hours, the disruptions of the past few days were set aside, and the afternoon proved to be a pleasant one, especially for the children. Toward the end, Debbie's eye became irritated from barbecue smoke, and David managed to get a nasty grease burn on one hand, and then a light drizzle put an end to the picnic.

It had been a carefree holiday outing and everyone was feeling good. The Glatzels were not prepared for the trouble that was waiting for them at home.

When they pulled into their driveway the night of July 4, it looked for a moment as though all the lights were on in the house. Yet, as they pulled up to the garage, the house stood dark and foreboding.

Carl Glatzel led the way inside. He refused to give credence to the "flighty" notions that his children and wife had spoken about. His attitude was one of complete and unswerving denial. Young Carl took his cue from his father and promptly followed him into the house.

The rest of the family followed, but David remained in the car. He knew something the others did not.

After about ten minutes Arne went out and found David sitting in the back seat of the station wagon.

"What's the matter?" Arne asked as he climbed in and sat beside David.

"The thing, the beast thing . . . it's inside the house. It got in through the attic. It's there right now," David said.

"What's it doing up there?"

"Waiting."

"No, I mean why is it there?"

"I told you before, it came to get me."

"Why you?"

"I don't know!"

It was hard for Arne to deal with the boy. Though David spoke with conviction, he was talking about something invisible, indeed something seemingly impossible. Arne was simply reduced to speaking on his level.

"David, even if the beast is up there, we're going to find a way to get rid of it. And with all of us around, he's not going to get to you. He's not going to take you anywhere. He'll have to go through me—he'll have to go through all of us first. Come on, let's go inside now."

"No way," David declared. "I'm not going in there. I'll sleep in the car. You don't understand what I'm talking about—none of you do. He wants to kill me—he said so!"

As Arne and David sat in the car, Carl Glatzel came out. He walked over to David's side of the car and opened the door. "Let's go, son. I want you in the house."

"No!" David said, disobeying his father for the first time in his life.

"Don't tell me no, David. Get your butt off that seat and march into the house or I'll pick you up and carry you in!"

David got out of the car and walked into the house with Arne and his father.

There was nothing perceptibly different inside the house. Jason, young Carl, and Carl, Sr., went to sleep early. David, however, refused to go to bed, and Judy allowed him to stay in the living room with the rest.

At about ten-thirty that night there were three

knocks at the front door. Judy assumed it was Pat Giddings and opened the door. Strangely, though, no one was at the door! Judy stepped outside to see if anyone was there, but all she heard were crickets chirping and frogs croaking in the front pond.

All was quiet for the next few minutes. Then they heard what sounded like barely audible scratching inside the livingroom wall. They listened intently for a minute.

Suddenly, an unmistakable *boom!* resounded in the attic. There was silence for a few seconds, then what sounded like footsteps walked across the attic floor above them.

"Arne," Judy said in a terrified whisper, "there's somebody up there!" Arne did not reply; he just continued listening to the noises.

Next, a muffled *boom-boom-boom* was heard downstairs in the kitchen. Then the scratching noise started again.

The scratching finally died away and all was quiet for the next five minutes. Then footsteps were heard again, this time walking forcefully across the attic floor. Then a series of delicate taps were heard hitting the living-room window.

Again, up in the attic, came a noise, something more than footsteps. Somebody was stomping across the attic with enough force to make the house vibrate.

"That's gonna wake your father up!" said Judy. "Arne, you better get ready to call the police. Carl won't fool around—he'll kill the guy."

They all waited to hear the bedroom door open, then for Carl Glatzel to appear. But he never came, though the stomping continued. Minutes later, however, Alan walked sleepily into the living room.

"Don't you hear it?" he asked. "Don't you hear those noises up in the attic?"

"We hear them," Arne said, rising out of the chair.

"Arne, where are you going?" Debbie asked, obviously worried.

"I'm going to find out what's up there," he said.

"Don't, Arne!" David pleaded. "There's no *person* up there. The beast is doing it!"

"Get me a flashlight," Arne said to Debbie.

Then he walked into the hall and pulled down the folding stairs to the attic. Judy handed him a flashlight, and with everyone standing at the base of the stairs, he climbed up.

Switching on the dim attic light, Arne saw only odd boxes and Christmas decorations. He trained the flashlight wherever something might be hiding, but there was nothing to be seen. Turning back, Arne heard what sounded like whisperings behind him. He swung around and stared in that direction, then walked directly to where he thought he'd heard the sounds come from. Goosebumps rose on his arms. Although it had been a hot summer day, the attic not only was cold, but the area in which he stood was even colder. Realizing there was nothing to be seen, Arne then climbed down the stairs. The fact that there was nothing to be seen or found, however, did not bode well.

Little did they know that they'd just experienced the first stage of diabolical manifestation.

Chapter VI

The heat wave was getting worse. High temperatures and oppressive humidity made each day more uncomfortable than the last. Air-conditioning was a necessity. However, during the night, the Glatzels' air-conditioning system had shut off.

When Carl Glatzel went down to the basement on the morning of July 5, 1980, he was prepared to perform major surgery on the unit. However, he discovered that the master switch had merely been moved to the "off" position. The basement doors were securely locked; who in the family could have done it? Carl reset the switch and the system kicked back in. Later, he asked everyone in the house if they had turned off the air-conditioner, but he got only denials. Their answers were unsatisfying, but he let the matter drop.

Carl had not heard the stomping noises in the attic the night before. When Judy told him what had happened, he simply asked, "Again?"

In fact, every few months over the past year or two, the whole family had been awakened at precisely three o'clock in the morning by violent poundings on the outside of the house. Judy recalled an incident when someone—or something—beat on their bedroom window so hard that it seemed the glass would break. On that occasion, Carl Glatzel got up, dressed, and went outside carrying a loaded shotgun, having every intention of using it. But, like all the other occasions, he never discovered who or what caused the noise.

Later that day, when the rest of the family was out of the house, Judy spoke with David. She wanted to get to the bottom of the problem.

"How do you feel, honey? Do you have a fever or anything?"

"I feel fine," David replied. "I've been fine."

"Tell me about this thing you've been seeing. What does it look like, and where is it now?"

"I'm not supposed to talk about him," David replied, "or he's gonna kill me, he said."

"Well, *I* want to know, and I'm your mother. You're my son and you have a right to talk to me."

"I don't know, mommy. I'm scared. The beast told me that he's now my father, and I'm only supposed to listen to him, and to say my prayers to him."

"What?" Judy was increduous.

"That's what he told me," David said. "And if I don't obey him, he said he's gonna have me stabbed; another time, he said he was gonna have me shot."

"Look, David," Judy countered, "I don't care what the beast says. You just answer my questions. First, I want you to tell me again what this thing looks like. And where is it now?"

"He's been over in the Giddings' basement all day. Since the waterbed is gone, he's taken over Debbie's mattress. He says he needs a place to relax. As for what he looks like, during the daytime he looks like an old man. He's got white hair and a mustache, and all the same clothes I told you about. Then at night he changes. He doesn't look like the old man anymore. I can't see him too clear, but his skin gets red all over. He's got a tail, and short horns come out of his forehead. I only see him kind of blurry that way, and he's never up close. When he's the old man, he says he hates my guts and is gonna destroy me. When he's red, at night, he's always saying how he's gonna 'fuck' someone. He thinks Mary is the most beautiful woman in the world, and he likes to be at the waterbed house because he likes to watch the girls without their clothes on. He's already touched their bodies when they're asleep."

"Why has it come to our house?" Judy asked.

"I asked him that," David revealed. "And he told me for two reasons. One was that he was going to retaliate against us for telling Mary Johnson he exists. But he also said he's been here a lot longer than we know."

Judy was more awe-stricken with every answer David gave, but she knew she must continue.

"The other day you said it had come to get you. Why has it picked on you? What have you done?"

"I don't know what I did. I didn't do nothin'," replied David. "The beast just said he wants a soul and he doesn't care whose it is. He said he's gonna get a soul, even if he has to *take* it."

"David, you've been reading your catechism, and you know that Jesus—"

"He says he's more powerful than Jesus," David interrupted, "and that he's in charge of the world. Oh no, Oh no . . ." David pulled back in the chair and stared with fright at something in the center of the room. Then he spoke as though there were someone present.

"I didn't meant to. . . . She told me to talk. . . . No . . . don't hit me!"

Suddenly Judy heard the sound of a loud slap, David's head spun to the side as a red mark appeared on his cheek. The event was incredible. She automatically jumped up and shouted angrily, "How dare you hit my son!"

A second later David was slapped in the face again.

"Don't mommy . . . don't talk back to him . . . please!"

Judy stood silent, fearing more would happen. But, having stopped the discussion then and there, no other unusual activity occurred that day.

That night, however, activity began again. There were scratching noises in the walls, and muffled poundings and sharp raps emanating from various spots in the house. Strangely, some sounds were heard by everyone, while other sounds were heard by only a few.

Both Carl, Sr., and Carl Jr., seemed to be "spared" the experience, save for the pounding noises. Young Carl was particularly eager to find the cause of the problem and went all over the house looking for the origin of the noises. He never found the source, and consequently accused David of playing a trick.

It was hard to know even where to look for the explanation to a phenomenon that had occurred earlier that afternoon. Judy, David, and Alan were working in the driveway when suddenly, in the middle of a still day, a gale-force wind blew through the trees, causing them to bend and sway. What struck everyone was that only the trees on their property were affected. All was still and serene on their neighbors' land. Most unsettling of all was David's announcement: "The beast just arrived." It was difficult to dispute his words.

That night, around ten o'clock, the intermittent noises stopped. The family went to bed shortly after eleven, and David, despite strong resistance, was made to lie in his own bed with the light off. He could not, however, fall asleep: a dread fear was building in him. David was sure something terrible was about to happen.

Alan and Jason were asleep, and David felt totally alone. He desperately wanted to get up, but was petrified to leave his bed, his only safe spot.

Then it began.

Daaaavid, said a low, strong voice from a distance. David's heart began to race.

Then he heard slow, heavy breathing in the room.

Daaaavid, the voice said again, only this time it seemed much nearer. David drew the covers up to his neck and stared out into the dark room. He knew what the voice was.

Daaaavid, the voice said even more clearly, and now obviously in the room. *I'm speaking to you, David. Answer me!* it commanded sharply.

David whimpered. "I hear you."

Can you see me, David?

"No."

Do you want to see me?

"No."

What you want is for me to go away, isn't it?

"Yes."

Then I will. I will go away forever. If you give me just one thing that I need. Will you give it to me?

David hesitated. "What do you want me to give you?"

Don't ask me questions, you scum! Just answer! Now, will you give me what I want? If you just say yes, I will always give you whatever you want, and you will never see me again. Is that not fair? Is that not what you want?

"Yes. I mean, no. I don't know what you want."

I want something you never use. Something you don't know you have. Something you will never miss. If you tell me no, I will never leave. You will always see me. And I will bring others with me. More hideous ones than you could ever think of. We will plague and torment you, always. Will you now say yes?

"I don't know what you want!"

I want your soul, David. Tell me yes and give it to me.

"My soul? Jesus says that the soul is God's most beautiful gift to people."

Do not talk to me of Jesus! Never say his fucking damn name in my presence or I will take care of Him. Now give me your soul, David. Now! Or you will see me! And I will take it!

David's mind was reeling. He said nothing.

David, sweetheart, I would not hurt you. I am your father. A father would not hurt his son. Come on. Don't say no to me! Say yes, David. Say yes!

Though he was only eleven, David held firm in his faith. "You are not my father! I will not give you my soul!"

There followed a moment of silence.

Then a reddish light began to fill the darkness in the center of the room. In the background David heard squealing and muted screaming. He sat up, his eyes riveted to the brightening red light.

A bizarre, powerful humming began to build, until David's hearing was totally overwhelmed by the sound. The unearthly noise continued to intensify until it was intolerable. And then—then it appeared.

What David saw was not the old man. What stood

58

before him, vivid and well-defined, slightly larger than a man, was distinctly a creature of diabolical order. It had scaly, light red skin and wore no clothes. It had a human male torso and stood on cloven feet. There were an odd number of clawed fingers on its hands. The thing had a tail. But it was to the face that David's attention was drawn. It was all white, with deep black eyes that looked like tunnels. The eye sockets were ringed with darkness. Horns protruded from the high forehead. It had pointed ears close to its bald head. The mouth was surrounded by a goatee and a drooping black mustache. The teeth were jagged and broken. The preternatural being stared at David in rage. In the distance, behind it, David vaguely saw two others!

Terrified, he let out a wild, bloodcurdling bellow, which woke up everyone in the house.

It took nearly ten minutes to calm David down sufficiently to speak.

"I saw him. . . . He showed himself to me. . . . Please . . . mommy, daddy . . . don't let him take me."

Carl Glatzel thought his son sounded like a hysterical idiot. Disgusted, he left the room, saying, "That's not my kid. Take him to a doctor. He's sick."

No one else felt that way—not even young Carl. David was exhibiting behavior so different from his ordinary, unsophisticated little-boy-personality that they could not fail to give credence to him.

Arne then took David into the living room so that he could sleep with him and Debbie. The other boys were sent back to their beds, with permission to keep the lights on.

Just after midnight, the poundings started again. Loud, hard, resounding wallops against the outside of the house.

Judy went into the bedroom to get Carl. But he refused to acknowledge the situation. He knew his family was terrified, but he simply told them to go to bed and ignore it. Judy left the bedroom, furious.

Walking down the hall to the living room, she felt something wet and slimy hit her bare arm.

"Can you see this thing? Is it in the house now?" she asked David.

"You just walked past it," he said. "He just spit on your arm."

"What happened to you before?" Judy asked. But David would not reply. "What happened to you in the bedroom, David?" she shouted. "Tell me!"

"He came, mommy. He came. He was all red. And mean. He said he wanted my soul."

Suddenly he stared fearfully at something in the room and began edging off the sofa, then moved slowly around the coffee table.

Incredibly, moments later, in full view of everyone, a forceful thud was heard, whereupon David went sprawling backward as though he'd been hit. He bounced off a chair and landed on the floor.

As soon as David was down, his head was knocked sharply to the right by some invisible force. He shouted in pain as he clutched his head with both hands.

Arne, Debbie, and Judy watched this spectacle in disbelief.

"The beast punched me," David muttered, sitting up, "then he kicked me in the head. . . ."

Smack! David's head again jerked to the side, apparently the result of a powerful slap in the face.

"My God!" Judy cried. "Stop that! Stop hitting my son, I command you!"

David, sitting on the floor, suddenly heaved forward with a load groan, as though he'd just been kicked in the stomach. Then as he leaned forward, he was knocked backward again from what seemed to be the force of a punch.

David rolled on the floor, doubled up in agony, "Don't *command* him no more," gasped David.

All stood appalled as David, panting, raised himself to a sitting position. His face and cheeks were suddenly swollen and red from the physical violence that was being inflicted on him.

"Where is it now, David?" Arne asked.

"Standing in the corner watching," David replied, regaining his breath.

"What does it want from us?" Judy asked desperately.

"I told you," said David. "He wants *me!*"

Judy sat down on the sofa, her head in her hands. Behind her, in the wall, the scratchings started again.

"Oh shut up!" she screamed at it. In reply, two muffled thuds sounded through the house.

"Don't talk to it, mommy," said David. "The beast is laughing at you real mean. He'll do it more."

David then raised himself off the floor and sat in a chair, rubbing his face with his fingers.

"Is this really happening?" Judy asked. "Or are we all imagining it, or dreaming, or what?"

"It feels real to me," David said with irony, bringing a brief, hard-won smile to his mother's face.

Although no one other than David had yet seen the physical manifestation of the entity, all felt its presence during the night. Judy's hair was pulled; Debbie's thigh was rubbed; Arne's wrist was grasped by a steel-cold hand. Sounds of movement were heard in the kitchen, and upstairs again in the attic.

But David was its prime victim. He *had* to watch it. He had to witness its hateful looks of scorn and rage. Most of all, he had to listen to the thing. From what the rest could understand, it constantly kept up a degrading harangue against the boy, either threatening him with physical punishment or seeking to break him down with vulgarities and accusations against both God and mankind.

David exhausted, began to nod off to sleep late in the night. But the moment he did, his head was lifted up by an invisible hand. When he opened his eyes, he gasped at the sight before him. It held his face so tightly his cheeks puckered. No one dared do or say anything, fearing that it would only result in more harm to David.

David was forced to be an intermediary, delivering messages from the entity and repeating the beast's replies. Attempts to communicate with the thing met only with profanity and unreason.

"Who are you?" yielded: *Suck my cock*.

"What is your name?" was answered: *None of your business*.

"Are you a ghost or a devil?" produced: *You'll find out*.

"Who sent you here?" earned the reply: *Your best friends*.

Debbie, asking, "Why don't you leave us in peace?" was told: *Get on your knees when you address me, you contemptible slut*.

By the time the sun rose, they all felt they'd aged a year. With the coming of light, David reported that the beast had returned *through* the ground to the rental property in Newtown. It did not, however, go to the house, David said. It went down into a deep well or septic tank behind the house, in the backyard, and from there it traveled out of the boy's sight below ground.

Before leaving Brookfield, though, the entity vowed it would return that night.

Chapter VII

When Carl Glatzel got up on Sunday morning, July 6, he found his wife fast asleep on the sofa, and his son David sleeping soundly on the floor between Arne and Debbie, who were still dressed in the clothes they'd worn the day before. Unaware of what had taken place during the night, he nonetheless took care not to wake them as he went into the kitchen and made a pot of coffee.

Eventually, young Carl, and then Alan, wandered into the kitchen.

"Remember last night after David yelled?" Alan said, sitting down at the table. "Well, after that he went into the living room, and something terrible must have happened, because about half an hour later, when Arne and Debbie and mom were with him, it sounded like somebody was getting beat up in there! I think it was David, because the other three kept saying stuff like, 'Help him, Arne,' and 'This can't be happening!' "

"I don't want to hear about it, Alan," Carl said.

"Shit, I told ya," Carl, Jr., gloated, "the bastards are all going whacko!"

"Carl, just shut your mouth!" his father ordered. "You sound as sick as the rest of them, and you've got yourself a real foul mouth, too! Where'd you get that dirty talk from, anyway? Curse one more time in this house and you're not going to eat for a week."

The smell of coffee and the loud talk in the kitchen roused the others, and the day began for the Glatzel family.

Yet, for those involved, what had happened the night before stayed with them—especially David, who had no way to flee. An otherwise beautiful day was already tainted with depression and gloom. Judy hoped this would change after they went to church.

As usual, Alan and David attended Mass Sunday morning with their mother. Young Carl, long refusing to go to church, always stayed home with his father, who was not religious. Arne, Debbie, and Jason, accompanied Judy and the two boys.

There was the usual flurry of activity before leaving. With everyone dressing at the same time, the only free mirror was the one in young Carl's room, so Debbie went there to brush her hair.

It is natural to feel safer in the light of day than in the dark of night. People somehow feel an immunity to evil in the daylight. Thus, as Debbie stood brushing her hair, she felt secure. But the feeling, was short-lived, as she realized she was not alone in the room.

A leather belt, draped across the top of the dresser, began slowly but discernibly to rise into the air in front of her. Debbie backed away with a gasp, watching as the belt levitated up some three feet, then turned vertically and dropped to the floor. The reality of an invisible presence in the room left her stiff with fright.

Just before they were all ready to leave, David announced that he was not going to church after all, admitting under pressure that the beast didn't want him to go.

To Judy, it was preposterous that she now had to compete for authority over her own child. Then at the door of the church, David again balked, claiming the beast had threatened him with "retaliation" if he went inside.

Judy, however, made sure he did go in and attend Mass. It was her only hope. But during Mass, David complained that a forceful hand kept pushing his head down, so that instead of being able to pay attention to the service, he was forced to bend over and stare at his shoes.

Judy felt the whole matter had gone too far. That afternoon, she and Debbie discussed the problem. Judy aired everything that was on her mind, including her fear that David was mentally ill.

"David was perfectly fine until July second," Debbie reminded her. She then told her mother about the levitation of the belt she'd witnessed that morning. "That was no mental problem of David's," Debbie declared, "it was a wholesale violation of the laws of nature."

Judy agreed that something extraordinary, but real, was occurring. "But what can we really do about it?" she asked.

David then came inside and said, "Mommy, the beast told me to tell you that he doesn't want you talking about ways to get rid of him. He says there's no way you're gonna get him out!"

"Who said that's what we were talking about?"

Judy asked, suppressing her astonishment. "Debbie and I were talking about baking cakes."

"No, you weren't," David insisted. "The beast has been in the house listening to you all the time. He told me what you said."

"He's in the house?" Judy asked angrily. "Where?"

"Right there, in the living room," David said without hesitation, "sitting in the rocking chair."

Judy quickly looked where David was pointing. "Good God," she whispered. The empty chair was rocking back and forth in the middle of the living room.

"All right, David, go back outside," Judy instructed.

Judy immediately went to her bedroom and got the small bottle of holy water, which she had refilled in church that morning. She cast a handful onto the rocking chair.

"In the name of Jesus, get out of this house and stay out!" she said vehemently. The rocking chair abruptly stopped moving.

"If that's what this thing understands, then I'll get a bucket of holy water and flush out the whole house," Judy vowed.

However, when she went back to her bedroom, she discovered that all her perfumes and cosmetics had been knocked over on the dresser. Judy and Debbie were astonished, then hit with fright.

"*Should* we see a priest?" Judy asked.

"And tell him what?" replied Debbie. "That you think you've got a ghost in the house? What makes you think they'd believe you? The Catholic Church doesn't even believe ghosts exist."

"This isn't my imagination: something *did* this!" Judy insisted, pointing at the top of the dresser.

"I know," Debbie said. "If this keeps up, we're going to have to get some kind of professional help.

Maybe the Church can help; I don't know. But I think it's too soon to be telling the priests at St. Joseph's that we think we've got spooks in our house. If you jump the gun, everyone in the family is liable to look like a turkey. We ought to hold off and see if anything else happens. Tomorrow, I'll talk to a few people at work and see if they have any idea what to do about this kind of problem."

"Well, you ask your questions," Judy said, "but if we go through another episode like last night, I'm going straight up to the rectory and talk to a priest."

That night at dinner, tempers flared as young Carl accused David of making up a ghost story to get attention, then accused the others of lying to protect him. He called Debbie a weasel for betraying Mary Johnson and the girls because Debbie "didn't like the color of the house." Finally, he threatened to "cripple" Debbie or Judy with his motorbike if he caught them in the driveway. The irrational arguing went on for hours. Caught up in anger and rage, there were times when young Carl couldn't even remember whom he was accusing, and would start off on a whole new course, sometimes flagrantly contradicting himself.

After the arguing died down that night, July 6, the house was deceptively still. Arne and Debbie stayed up late, discussing their own problems. Deciding not to stay at the rental house had left them broke and had alienated them from Mary and the girls. But they thought perhaps things had changed, and maybe Mary was ready to move now. Therefore, they decided to stop by the rental house after work the next day and find out.

Suddenly, as they talked, David began moaning, turning his head in his sleep. The moans soon changed to audible words: "help . . . run . . . no . . . no . . . help me . . ." Arne and Debbie stared at David as his torso began to shake. They heard a gale wind blowing through the trees, but when Debbie looked out the front window, all was still.

Moments later, they heard something being dropped on the floor of the attic. David opened his eyes, rose from the sleeping bag, and stared speechlessly at Arne and then at Debbie.

"David, you with us, buddy?" Arne asked. Rigid with fear, David simply nodded. Gooseflesh rose on their arms as they heard what seemed to be a group of people walking around in the attic.

The hall light suddenly switched on. But it was only Judy coming into the living room, half-asleep.

"What's going on?" she asked, squinting in the light. "Did you hear the footsteps in the attic?"

"It's the beast," David announced. "In my sleep I saw him come shooting straight up out of the well behind Mary's house. He went high above the trees, carrying something—boxes. Then he flew over here in a shot. He brought the boxes to our house." As he spoke, he stared up toward the attic.

"Boxes?" Judy questioned. "What kind of boxes?"

"There's three boxes," David said. "They're regular-sized. One is red, one is black, and one is yellow."

"What's in them?"

"I don't know what's in them!" David answered crossly. "They're closed. He's just walking around them in circles."

"I don't hear any walking," Debbie said firmly. "Do you, mom?" Judy shook her head.

"David, I'm not convinced there's any 'beast' here," Debbie asserted. "If he's so almighty powerful, tell him to prove himself. Tell the thing to prove it's here by flashing the lights on and off!"

70

"Please, Debbie—don't! He hates being questioned. You're gonna make him do something bad," David said.

"I don't give a damn what he's gonna do! If he's really here, and he's so powerful, just tell him to make the lights flash on and off. *Or maybe he can't?*"

Debbie got her answer. The living-room lights dimmed, went off momentarily, then flashed on and off three times. The demonstration was sobering.

"The beast says, 'How would you like to hear some knocking?' " said David.

Four knocks sounded. They seemed to emanate from the living-room floor.

"This is too much!" Debbie cried.

"I told you not to tempt him," David said matter-of-factly.

The knocking continued until Debbie capitulated and said, "All right! All right! Tell him to stop."

A few more knocks were heard. "Did he answer you, David?" Debbie asked.

"Yeah, but it was dirty."

"I don't care; tell me what the beast said," Debbie insisted, as the knocking continued.

"He said . . ." The knocking grew louder. "He said, 'Fuck you,' " David replied hesitantly.

The irritating knocks came to an end as each person sat silently trying to understand what was happening.

After five minutes, David broke the silence: "He's opening up one of the boxes now—the black one.

"He's got the top of it open. . . . A whole bunch of bugs flew out. . . . Now he's pushing the box over on its side. There's something inside it. . . . Snakes . . . a bunch of snakes just tumbled out."

David stopped, and Judy asked, "Anything more?"

"That's it," he replied, still staring at the same spot above him, "except there were a lot of little snakes that seemed to come together and turn into a couple of big snakes . . . two. . . . Now there's none, and the beast is laughing. They became something else, I don't know what. . . . He's talking to whatever it is, but I can't understand the language."

"I want this to stop," Judy declared. "Just ignore the thing, like your father says."

"I can't help it, mommy. He keeps talking to me. And cursing at me. And telling me to *give in*."

"David, please, son, just lie down and close your eyes and try not to hear it," Judy pleaded.

The knocking started again.

"The beast just warned me he's not done yet," David said, looking at his mother. "He said he's brought my punishment and that I'm going to wish I was never born."

"You tell that beast thing if he tries to hurt you—if he even lays a hand on you—I'll have a priest in this house at the crack of dawn!" Judy threatened.

At David's request, Judy agreed to stay all night with them again in the living room.

Eventually, they all fell asleep, but shortly before three that morning they were awakened by a sonic vibration that slowly intensified to a low-pitched roar. The humming—like that of an electric turbine—kept getting louder until it was the only thing any of them could hear. The vibrations set pencils, paper clips, and other small objects in the room into frenetic motion.

What was happening?

Why was it happening?

The whirring roar seemed to penetrate the very flesh with its powerful vibration.

Then, abruptly, it stopped.

At least the noise stopped. For David, it marked the arrival of a whole new form of terror—one he could not even imagine. At precisely the moment the humming stopped, David's attention was drawn to the doorway. He was so overwhelmed that he couldn't even scream.

What appeared before the boy was not only the deranged countenance of the beast; with it were two additional abominations.

One stood to the left of the beast, the other at the right, and each was uniquely gruesome.

The new entities were tall and thin, with wiry arms that ended in stubby, clawlike fingers. Their skin was red. Both stood on cloven feet. Like the beast, they had horns protruding from their heads. The horns of one entity were pointed and no more than an inch long. The other entity's horns were more fulsome, like those of a steer, and projected from the sides of its head. Though their appearance was half-man and half-animal, the entities were not identical. They were "individuals," with humanoid features. What immediately distinguished the two were the wounds: one had a bullet hole in the center of its forehead, and its face was covered with blood; the other had a knife stuck in its chest directly where the heart should be.

Like the beast, they looked crazed and wild. Their eyes moved independently of each other, sometimes crossing, sometimes directing a hypnotizing gaze at David. As they looked at the boy dispassionately, they spoke about one thing only: his soul.

David, completely overwhelmed by what he had seen, managed to utter only three words: "He's got helpers!"

Chapter VIII

Was David having hallucinatory delusions? Was the whole family experiencing mass hysteria? Might it be a collective dream? Or was there nothing wrong with them at all? Could their experiences be valid? Was this, in fact, the real thing?

These were among the questions Judy Glatzel struggled with when David related, with conviction and sincerity, what he claimed to have witnessed the night before. Judy knew almost nothing about spirit phenomena, so she had to depend on her common sense.

And Judy's common sense told her that her family was undergoing a very strenuous, very real ordeal, full of bizarre and terrifying occurrences.

What disturbed Judy most were David's descriptions of entities with horns and hooves and strange red skin. He was describing a stereotypical devil. It was too corny. If anything, these descriptions dissuaded her from believing the spirit-phenomena theory.

Judy needed someone to talk to. She needed more information. Something had to happen, one way or the other, to demonstrate to her satisfaction whether the matter was mental or spiritual in origin, so that she could act accordingly and put a stop to it.

At four-thirty, Arne and Debbie came home from work. Both were fatigued and dirty: fatigued from being up half the night, and dirty from their work at the Canine 21 Kennels. While Debbie was taking a shower, Judy asked Arne if they'd stopped to see his mother. The question obviously upset him. Yes, he told Judy, they had, and it had been a disaster. His mother had seemed almost possessed in her anger at him and Debbie and had virtually disowned them both.

Arne and Debbie had tried to tell her about the trouble they'd experienced in Brookfield during the week and to warn her again of the potential danger there. But Mary Johnson would have no part of it. She told them that absolutely nothing had happened in the rental house and that the "foolish" talk about ghosts had only scared the girls. Debbie and Arne did not know that Mary was lying to them: she and the girls had been having problems in the house from the very first day.

When Debbie was done with her shower and came into the kitchen, she said, "You're not gonna believe this, but when I got undressed in the bathroom, something began to stroke my thigh. I really felt it! I actually turned around to see if someone was in there with me." Judy and Arne didn't even comment.

When Arne went to take his shower, Judy asked Debbie if she had gotten any information from her coworkers.

"It was a hard subject to bring up," Debbie said, "but I managed to have a long conversation with Melissa, the other dog groomer."

"Is she a psychic or something like that?" asked Judy.

"No, but she knows about the subject. She knew some people who had some really hairy experiences with a ghost a few years ago, and they got help from people named Warren, who got rid of the ghost for them. I've got the name written down."

Judy felt a sudden ray of hope. "I've heard about the Warrens. They're supposed to be good. Did Melissa know how to get hold of them?"

"She didn't know anything other than their name. Her suggestion was to ask around."

At that moment, Pat Giddings knocked on the back door and let herself in. Pat, a year younger than Debbie, is thin, with wild blond hair and a pleasant face.

"Hi! Want to go shopping with me tonight, Deb?" she asked.

"I can't," Debbie said. "I'm dead tired, and I want to go to sleep early."

"What's the matter—are you sick? You look awful!" Pat said with obvious concern.

"You wouldn't believe it if I told you."

"Try me," Pat said, sitting down at the table.

Debbie told her the basic story, starting with the incident on the waterbed and working up to the fact that they now felt there was reason to believe they had a ghost, or spirit, or something, in the Brookfield house with them.

Pat Giddings listened with a grave face. "What time did you say you heard the wind blowing last night?" she asked.

"Around midnight," Debbie replied, "but I didn't see any movement outside to back up what I heard."

"Well, I did," Pat revealed. "I went to bed at quarter to twelve. Around midnight I heard a terrific

77

wind pick up. I got up and looked out the window. The wind was blowing like crazy and the trees were bending and twisting like a storm was going on. Then the wind died down and everything returned to normal. It was unusual—enough to get me out of bed—but at the time it didn't mean anything to me."

"Uh-oh! Your stuff is in our basement. Ever since you put it down there, my kids won't go into the cellar. They say they're afraid. And I've heard movements down there! A couple of times this week I could have sworn somebody was down there. In fact, right now that mattress you propped up against the wall between the boxes is lying flat out on the floor. I don't know how it got there. Ted [Pat's husband] wouldn't have done it."

"We know why the mattress is on the floor," Debbie said. She then explained how David had alleged that the so-called ghost man used it to relax on.

Pat asked that Debbie and Arne take the mattress out of her basement immediately. Debbie and Arne then dragged it back across the lawn and leaned it up against the side of the Glatzels' house. Before separating that evening, Pat offered to do anything she could to help. Her gracious offer was a mistake: she would regret it.

While Debbie and Arne were moving the mattress, Judy began cooking dinner. As she stood at the sink, she had the unmistakable feeling that someone was behind her. Not only did she feel crowded, she felt the light sensation of someone breathing on the back of her neck. Without looking, she stepped back quickly, to test her hunch, but bumped into nothing. Then she glanced around, but no one was there.

A moment later, Judy felt a hard pinch on her derriere. She spun around and, without thinking, said, "Keep your dirty hands off me!"

Instantly, Judy realized what she'd done. Something had *caused* her to respond.

Judy was tired of doubting herself and her perceptions. Something really was happening. Suddenly she felt alone in a house full of danger. Then it occurred to her how David must feel. His frantic behavior was based on the fact that he was terrified! Judy suddenly realized she had to stop her incessant questioning of David, and change her skeptical attitude to a more sympathetic one.

Fatigued from being up night after night, Arne, Debbie, Judy, and David were ready for sleep by eleven o'clock. As usual, they slept in their clothes. One light was left on as a precaution.

A few minutes after they settled down, Alan and Jason came into the living room with their pillows and insisted on sleeping there. They said they'd heard "funny sounds" in the closet near their beds. David, not wanting to scare them, didn't say that during the day the beast had moved the two unopened boxes out of the attic and into the bedroom closet.

Soon David began complaining that one of the three entities kept poking him every time he closed his eyes. And when he opened them, he reported, they kept cursing at him and threatening him with death. The harassment continued without let-up for an hour. No one knew what to do.

Knockings on the coffee table then started up. The sound of a fist pounding on the wall was added. David yelped with fright as, he claimed, an entity suddenly rushed up on him, stopping precisely at the point of his nose.

Finally, Arne told David to say, "Jesus is Lord and the Lord will protect me."

"Jesus is Lord and the Lord will protect me," David dutifully repeated.

The next word out of his mouth was *Help!*

In the next second, David Glatzel found himself lying helplessly on his back. His legs kicking, his body squirming, his tongue hanging out, he was actually in the throes of being choked!

Out of nowhere, David was engaged in a struggle for his life as he desperately tried to pull two unseen hands away from his throat.

Then, before anything could be done to help him, the attack was over.

David lay flat on his back, panting and coughing, until he was finally able to draw a few deep breaths. Visible on his neck were unmistakable impressions of fingers!

David was not attacked again that night. But, under the circumstances, it was impossible and unwise for the others to sleep.

The next day, Judy was exhausted and cranky. When young Carl launched into David for "seeing things," Judy went at him like an enraged tiger. Carl, Jr., argued back fiercely and viciously, ultimately calling his mother a "goddamn bitch who ought to be killed" and suggesting that he'd be the one to do it.

During the afternoon, Judy tried to get David to describe precisely what had happened during the choking incident. He seemed totally intimidated by the forces at work. All he would tell his mother was that the helpers were stationed at the front and back doors and that the beast was in the room, standing behind him. David said this while finishing off a soup bowl full of ice cream and a dozen chocolate cookies. Watching David mechanically send cookies down his throat like a gambler feeding quarters into a losing slot machine, Judy realized why there was almost nothing left to eat in the house. For the past week, David had become obsessed with eating.

Judy no longer had any doubts as to the cause of the problem. The appalling spectacle of her son being almost choked to death for speaking about Jesus had pushed her beyond the brink. Thus, on July 8, Judy began the process of seeking help.

Judy had to find someone who knew about spirit phenomena and could tell her how to eliminate the problem. She tried to find a phone number or address for the Warrens, whom she knew had expertise in the subject, but she reached a dead end.

Next, she decided to call Father Dennis, an older priest who was working with David on his catechism, so he could make his First Holy Communion. Judy dialed the rectory, then had second thoughts. What could she say to Father Dennis? What kind of proof could she give? Judy hung up on the first ring and made no more calls that day.

Later, after dinner, tempers again flared. As usual, young Carl made preposterous accusations, against which the others sought to defend themselves. Arne, though he too was verbally attacked, did not get involved in the sparring. Nor would David join in. As Arne discovered, David knew something the others did not.

Over the shouting, Arne asked, "Where's the beast thing right now, David?"

"In the kitchen, standing behind little Carl."

"And where are the helpers?"

"They're in the kitchen too," David said, as though it were obvious.

"What are they doing in there?"

81

"The beast is staring a hole through little Carl's head, and the helpers are by the refrigerator, laughing like crazy at everyone."

"Did they start this argument?"

"They started it all right," David said flatly. "They start them all."

Until the night of July 8, no one else had seen what David had been calling the beast. That night, Debbie witnessed it for herself.

The arguing that night eventually came to an end, but the words left their wounds nonetheless. Afterward, Debbie felt like she was being followed around, and it set her on edge. She was petrified of being stuck alone where some malign force might corner her.

But it didn't happen that way. Instead, while watching television, with Judy, David, Alan, and Arne in the room, Debbie happened to notice movement above her. She looked up and, without saying a word, stared at the ceiling. No one noticed Debbie's predicament until half a minute later, when David saw what was happening. He went over to the couch where Debbie was sitting.

"Debbie," said David. "Come on, Debbie. Stop looking at it." She did not, however, yield.

David put his hands on her head and forced it down, thereby breaking her trance.

Debbie looked wide-eyed at her brother. "David, this thing, this beast—does he have high cheekbones, a long nose, pointed ears, and black, black eyes that draw you into them?" David nodded. "And he *does* have horns, doesn't he? And a goatee, and a mustache?"

"Yes. I saw him looking at you, too," David said. "That's why I came and got you."

For Debbie Glatzel, it was not a matter of how it looked, but rather what happened when she looked at it. When Debbie made eye contact with the thing, a horrid terror rose inside her. She felt herself either being uncontrollably drawn toward the thing, or else the thing was beginning to flood into her. Either way, she wanted to scream that it was taking her over, but she had no voice with which to do it.

Chapter IX

The gravity of the situation hit Judy the next morning, July 9, when she went into the rectory of Saint Joseph's Church in Brookfield. Amid the somber trappings of the rectory waiting room, Judy's stomach tightened. The room smelled faintly of church incense. On the wall across from her hung a large wooden crucifix, reinforcing the solemnity of her visit.

There was no doubt in Judy's mind that she should be sitting there. It had been a night of absolute hell.

She had been forced to watch helplessly, along with Arne, Debbie, and Alan, as David was slapped, punched, and kicked repeatedly. Replaying it in her mind, Judy could hear the hard slaps and David's cries of pain when he refused to renounce God and pledge his soul to the entities.

"Say what they want if it'll make them stop!" Judy had told him. But David refused. Then David had yelled in terror, "Help me, mommy! He's got a pistol! He's going to shoot me!"

They'd heard everything but the report of the gun, as David was blown backward and, clutching his stomach, keeled over on the kitchen floor as though dead.

Judy remembered the look of desperation on Arne's face as he reported no breathing, no pulse, no heart-beat coming from her son's body. And, after that, her gratitude when David suddenly opened his eyes.

Fatigued and wrenched with emotion, Judy's only hope was that the Church could stop the bedlam being inflicted on her family.

Ten minutes after she'd arrived, Father Dennis took Judy into his small, book-filled office and shut the door. The priest's comfortable manner and gentle voice immediately put her at ease. In his early sixties, with graying hair and a gentle tone of voice, Father Dennis was the pastor of St. Joseph's Church in Brookfield. His peers have called him a priest's priest. Father liked the pace and quality of life in Brookfield, and Brookfield liked him too. On the occasion of his thirty-fifth anniversary as a priest, the town proclaimed May 15, 1977, "Father Dennis Day".

For the next half-hour, Judy told Father Dennis the impossible problem her family had been living with.

She told him about the gruesome entities David had been seeing and recounted his descriptions of their appearance. She told him about the knockings, the rappings, the footsteps, the arguing, the anger, the predictions, and the terror it had all evoked. She told Father Dennis that her family had become victims of forces that she could scarcely comprehend.

Father Dennis told Judy that he had heard of such things before. He explained that there could be a vari-ety of causes for the phenomena, including psychological instability, but he would need more information before coming to any judgment. He did not know why such an assault might be launched against her family, but suggested there was almost always an origin to these matters—one based either on something that they'd done, or on something that had been done to them.

As Judy answered in detail the questions that the priest put to her, she was trembling inside. Father Dennis wasn't telling her what she wanted to hear. Judy wanted him to say, "Don't be silly. Such things don't exist." But it wasn't to be.

"Then it's possible that David really is being set upon by these spirits?" she summoned the courage to ask.

"I would have to speak with David," Father Dennis replied.

"But you're telling me that these things *do* happen— or at least they have happened before?"

"Historically, yes, there is certain precedent for it. But I'm afraid you underestimate the complexity of the world, Mrs. Glatzel."

Judy then began asking deeper questions that had been troubling her all along.

"What kind of spirits would these be, providing, of course, that they're there? Would they be ghosts?"

"I have no way of knowing," the priest told her honestly. "But let me remind you that the Church recognizes only two types of spirits: the spirits of good, and the spirits of evil."

"Father, David is talking about seeing entities with horns and hooves and all the markings of a devil. Honestly, I have a lot of trouble believing that; in fact, I have to say it even causes me to doubt my son, in part, though I know he isn't lying. I just can't make any sense out of it."

Father Dennis was reluctant to say more, but the woman before him was obviously in great distress. He suggested that if the problem was psychological, his coming to the house might only fuel the child's fantasy. Therefore, he told Judy to take a half-dozen holy candles home with her and place them around the house. If the problem was truly spiritual in nature, the candles would be anathema to the suspected entities and might cause them to leave. If the candles worked, they would both know why. If the candles did not work and trouble started again, Judy was to call him.

With great hope, Judy took the big red-glass church candles home, and placed one in each room of the house, and lit them. For the time being, the gesture was both helpful and reassuring.

Meanwhile, that Wednesday, July 9, was Jason's seventh birthday. Judy directed her attention to the simple pleasure of baking a birthday cake and preparing a party for him later in the afternoon.

The birthday party was a pleasant respite. For a brief time they lived like normal people. Jason's favorite present was an eighteen-inch-tall model dinosaur from Arne and Debbie. The only sour incident during the day occurred when flashbulbs went off in Arne's hand as he was about to take photographs of the party.

It was hoped the church candles would finally restore tranquility to the home, which they appeared to do—until midnight.

Then it started again. There were three ominous knocks at the front door, followed by hard, sharp raps on the outside of the house. Inside, something was felt moving around the living room, turning that area of the room cold wherever it was.

At dawn, David claimed that the beast and his two helpers had spent most of the night jeering and laughing at him. David said he had also been threatened with more shootings and violence because of his mother's trip to the rectory and for having the holy candles in the house.' The child was also told that if *he*—whoever that might be—came to the house the next day, David would get a surprise he'd never forget.

The "he" in question turned out to be Father Dennis, whom Judy called the following afternoon.

David had been tormented all night and into the morning. Young Carl was out of control, fighting and arguing with his brothers continuously. Jason came limping into the house with a bruised ankle, complaining that something had kicked him. Judy's hair had been pulled. There were knocking sounds and unintelligible whisperings. A cold presence was stationed in the hallway, blocking access to the boys' rooms. And something in the house had physically picked up one of the lighted holy candles and thrown it against the living-room wall, splattering red wax everywhere. Judy's cosmetics had again been knocked over, and on her clean white bedspread were series of sooty, *cloven footprints*!

Father Dennis was there within ten minutes of Judy's call. Activity ceased when he arrived. Nonetheless, Judy took the priest into the master bedroom and showed him what remained of the cloven footprints on the bedspread, which were then fading away.

But it was to David that Father Dennis wanted to speak. He felt that the child might be imagining much of what he claimed to see. As a teacher, he knew that a sharp child in a boring environment sometimes fabricates substitute realities as an expression of deeper psychological distress. However, after hearing David's account of what had been occurring, Father Dennis told Judy that he felt the best procedure would be for him to bless the house and fill it with "the Aura of

Christ." Obviously, the priest believed there were valid spirit phenomena occurring in the Glatzel house.

Father Dennis went out to his car and brought in his black traveling bag. From it he took a long purple stole, and after kissing the fabric placed it around his neck. He then took out a brass aspergillum and a water container with a cross on it. Next, in Latin, he recited a blessing over the water.

Beginning in the basement and working up to the attic, Father Dennis blessed every room in the house. It was not an exorcism of the dwelling—that was a far more specific and complicated procedure requiring some considerable preparation by the priest—but rather a dedication of the home to the spirit of God. Father Dennis knew that if lesser entities were involved, the blessing would keep them out. Stronger, more malevolent spirits, however, would be inclined to disobey the commands of God. In such circumstances, though, prudence dictates that conservative procedures be employed first, reserving more radical procedures for when they are needed.

Finally, he put a protective blessing on David, and recommended that in the evening the family, together as a group, recite the Our Father and the Prayer to Saint Michael, both of which contain repudiations of evil. In the event that the phenomena started again, they were to read aloud Psalm 23 as well.

That night, serenity had seemed at last to have descended on the Glatzel home. The beast and its two macabre helpers, reported David, had floated back over the treetops to the rental house in Newtown.

Even Carl Glatzel, Sr., expressed amazement that the pressure was off since the priest had come. Everything was suddenly normal and plans were made for a family outing that weekend.

All were again physically and mentally fatigued from the long, disquieting episode, and bedtime came early. David slept in his own room with Alan and Jason and didn't even ask for a nightlight. Judy returned to her husband's side, and Arne and Debbie began to think of a new beginning in their lives.

On the way to work the next day, Arne told Debbie that during the night he'd had the distinct impression that something—or someone—was standing over him, staring, and that he had stayed awake until dawn for fear something might happen.

It was David, however, who related the most incredible story the next afternoon. At three o'clock David came into the house to get a glass of water. On the floor near the refrigerator was the big model dinosaur that Jason had gotten for his birthday. The toy was "authentic in every detail"—with movable joints and a hinged jaw.

When David turned around from the sink, he was shocked. The model dinosaur had *come to life!*

Aghast, David watched as the nearly two-foot-tall toy took a few steps toward him and stopped.

Its right front leg swiveled up and pointed at David. With its hinged jaw moving, it said, *Beware! You will be stabbed!* The plastic beast then went still.

David ran out of the house in a frenzy. Not only had the toy moved; not only had he been threatened with further violence; but this meant the spirits were back! Judy, however, refused to believe that notion. It was over, she insisted. Over!

When David went to bed that night, he did so with great trepidation. He couldn't sleep. He lay in the dark room, wide awake and alert. At first he simply felt uneasy; that emotion, however, slowly transformed into one of foreboding. Deep down, David knew something awful was about to happen.

Shortly after midnight it did. What arrived, one by one, were emissaries from the devil.

First came the beast. It walked through the wall as though it didn't exist and stood, in all its wicked glory, at the foot of David's bed. It was out of its mind with fury. The priest's blessing had affronted its power.

You bastard! You stinking human being! You betraying scum! How dare you insult me! I am the Power! I am all there is! There is no God! God is shit! You are shit!

Its eyes were wild as it proceeded into blasphemies against the priest and the whole "unfair" kingdom of God.

As the beast entity carried on with its awful fulminations, the two bloody helpers arrived. They materialized slowly until they appeared as solid as the first entity. Then they too began screaming and raging at the child.

Debilitated with fright, David sought to cry out for help, but he had no voice. The madness went on and on. Sometimes they spat out accusations so fast that David couldn't follow what they were saying. Sometimes they spoke in languages he didn't understand. And many times what they said made no sense to him.

We will make you one of us.

Long have you been ours.

We own your soul.

For hours, blasphemy, profanity, commands, demands, threats, predictions, wailing, screaming, and bloodcurdling shrieks flowed continuously. The degradation was total.

What more could possibly happen?

David Glatzel found out. When he did, he almost fainted.

The beast and its two helpers began a profane chant and repeated it monotonously many times. Soon David noticed the appearance of a blueish ball of light manifest in the vicinity of the three chanting spirits.

The ball of light grew radiant, then elongated into a pencil-thin beam, which broadened out to the size of a man. The beam grew vivid in detail until a fourth entity materialized in the room! Once manifest, the creature was hideous in every way. It stood over six feet tall, and had one eye in the front of the head and one eye in the back. Its nose was cut off, its mouth ripped open. Its flaring red body was lacerated with slash marks out of which oozed blood. It had a gaping hole in its stomach. It appeared to be insane.

The three original entities laughed evilly as other balls of light began to move ominously around the room. Then, another of the golf-ball-sized lights began the materialization process, resulting in a fifth entity. This one was completely black and totally repugnant. Its body was burned and it appeared to have been cremated.

To this spectacle of three beserk, laughing entities and two recently materialized monsters was added a sixth. This corruption stood over eight feet tall, and with only one eye, looked neither like man nor animal though it too stood on cloven feet and had horns protruding from its skull.

Then a seventh entity showed, perhaps even more ghastly than the rest. This entity's head was split open in the middle, as was its face. Blood dripped down from the eyes. It had one arm and only three fingers. One leg had a hoof; the other leg was cut off two inches below the knee.

David was terrified as groups of inhuman beings

began to materialize. Some had lizard-like features, while others had small heads with grotesque protruding snouts like gargoyles. Some of their bodies were half-burned; others had eyes gouged out or limbs hacked off; yet others were cadaverous and desiccated, with protruding bones and skulls. And still they kept coming, with ghastly disfigurements and distortions of the face, body, and limb. Indeed, what David saw was no less than a *legion* of devils!

In all, forty new entities appeared that night.

Each was a unique, individual monstrosity.

Worst of all, every one of them would stay.

Chapter X

The next morning, Saturday, Judy listened with grief and anger as David related the havoc he had witnessed during the night.

Judy called Father Dennis immediately and told him what had happened. The priest arrived at the house within an hour of Judy's summons.

Father Dennis knew what was occurring in the Glatzel house. He had seen it before and he knew the solution. But he was not the man for the job. His health was bad: a year earlier he had collapsed during Mass, and he had never fully regained his vitality. Furthermore, he was not an exorcist, in the classical sense. He had successfully performed the function in the past, but any attempt on his part to expel the very powerful inhuman forces from the Glatzel home could lead to his own death. The other priests in the rectory had advised him to "go slow" on the matter, but they had no experience with the subject. Father Dennis was therefore carrying the load alone.

When Father Dennis arrived at the Glatzel home that afternoon, all were waiting for him in the living room—except Carl, Sr., who was at work, and Carl, Jr., who stayed outside and laughed scornfully at the rest.

"This isn't the first time this sort of thing has happened in this part of Connecticut," Father Dennis told the Glatzels. "The way to put an end to it is through strict religious procedures." He explained that his next step would be to refer the matter to the Diocese of Bridgeport, which would have to assign the proper clergy to the case to help bring the matter to a conclusion. In the meantime, the priest said, the Glatzels could do something for themselves. Church officials would require investigation and verification of the case before action would be taken. The process could take a long time—even months. To expedite the process, he recommended that the family call in Ed and Lorraine Warren, investigators who were experienced in the theological ramifications of spirit phenomena and whose judgment would be accepted by Church officials.

Father Dennis did not tell Judy that the Warrens' work was in the area of demonology. He referred to them under the nebulous term *psychic investigators*, which made it easier for Judy to accept.

Although Judy had vainly hoped for an instant solution, she now felt at least some progress was being made. It struck her as important that for the second time the Warrens were recommended as the experts whom she should contact. Pat Giddings told Judy that the Warrens lived in Connecticut and that when she spoke with her mother-in-law the next day she would be able to get the Warrens' phone number.

For the Glatzels, a day was a long time. And when night came, David reported that the many spirits he'd seen the previous night were now beginning to congregate around him in the room. Their appearance was intimidating. But even more so were the whips and clubs they were carrying.

Throughout the long night, David was tormented with the threat of violence. The bloody ghouls would approach the boy with clubs or steel bars in their claws, and go through all the preparatory motions of delivering a killing blow. David would wince and cower, much to the horror of his family.

Suddenly, David exclaimed, "The helpers—they've got knives!" There was no place for David to hide as the entity with the bullet hole in its head and the one with the knife stuck in its heart came forward from the pack, each brandishing a long-bladed steel kitchen knife.

At four o'clock in the morning, on July 13, David was stabbed. It was the fulfillment of the prediction made two days before, through the agency of the model dinosaur.

One entity stabbed David in the back, while the other stabbed him in the side.

The family watched, appalled, as David folded to the floor with a desperate groan. Above him, beyond the reach of human sight but plainly visible to David, stood the two inhuman assailants, cursing him and jeering while the child apparently lay dying.

Arne tore open David's shirt. To everyone's relief, he found no bleeding wounds. There were, however, two slender red marks, one on his right side and another in the center of his back.

David's pain was excruciatingly real to him. But gradually the intensity of the pain diminished, and fifteen minutes later he felt only soreness. The stabbing put an end to the activity that morning, but the effects lingered in everyone's mind.

Next to Judy, Arne was the most affected by the

constant assaults on David. He did everything he could to protect the boy, including covering him with his own body to take the beatings himself. Unlike everyone else, Arne expressed no fear of the beast and its deranged cohorts. Indeed, he challenged them.

"Do it to me!" Arne shouted at the entities. "I'll take your punches, the kid can't defend himself." But, David reported, they only laughed at Arne with derision.

Later that Sunday came perhaps the first positive development toward solving the problem. Pat Giddings had gotten the Warrens' phone number through her mother-in-law, who knew of the Warrens not just because of their role as investigators of the Amityville case on Long Island, but because they've been the people to call for the past thirty-five years when one moves into a haunted New England House. Fortunately, the Warrens lived only thirty minutes away from Brookfield Center.

At ten o'clock that Sunday night, July 13, 1980, Pat called the Warrens on behalf of her friends, Carl and Judy Glatzel. In a tense, strained voice, she gave a detailed account of the havoc her neighbors were experiencing in their Brookfield home, and asked if the Warrens could help them.

Ed and Lorraine Warren, each listening on an extension, absorbed the young woman's narrative, then told her that, for legal reasons, the Glatzels would have to call them directly. The Warrens suggested that Pat have someone in the Glatzel family call back.

Lorraine Warren had only one comment to her husband when they hung up the phone: "Brookfield. I told you!"

Ten minutes after Pat spoke with the Warrens, Judy Glatzel called them. The Warrens asked Judy a preliminary run of questions. Judy rattled off the incredible list of events that had gone on since July 2, and capped it off with the allegation that there were forty-three different entities involved, one of which declared it wanted David's soul. Judy also told the Warrens that she'd talked at length with Father Dennis in Brookfield, who had found it necessary to formally bless their house.

"Has a doctor seen the child yet?" Ed asked.

"He's regularly seen by a pediatrician," Judy replied, "but David's not sick, so his doctor doesn't know about this."

"If we came tonight, would you mind if we brought a medical doctor along with us?"

"Please—bring anybody you want who can help," Judy said, relieved that progress was being made.

The Warrens took the Glatzels' address and phone number and said they'd be there within an hour.

The time was 10:30 P.M.

Just as Judy hung up the telephone, an agonized scream came from the boy's bedroom. Debbie and Judy ran in and found Jason on the floor, twisting his head back and forth. Tears flowed down his cheeks.

"I fell down," Jason sobbed. "Something pushed me off the top bunk, and I landed on my head."

"David, do you know anything about this?" Judy asked sternly.

"Jason was up there telling me that he felt a hand touching him today, and this morning that hand grabbed his ankle and made him trip. The beast was standing here listening, and got mad all of a sudden at Jason for telling me what happened. He said, '*You little shit,*' to Jason, and then went over and pushed him off the bed so he'd get hurt."

"Where's the beast now?"

"In the living room," David replied, "sitting on the

99

couch next to little Carl. Carl can't hear him, but the beast is telling him to make trouble tonight."

"And where are all the helpers?"

"Waiting outside," David answered. "The beast sent them out there to watch for the people you called, the Warrens, and a man named Dr. Tony, who he says they're gonna pick up. He says we're gonna be sorry they came and he'll turn the Warrens' life upside down if they try to interfere."

In response to Judy's call, Ed and Lorraine Warren contacted Father Dennis at St. Joseph's rectory at 10:35 P.M. The Warrens already knew the priest and had great respect for him. Father Dennis confirmed that he had been giving counsel to the Glatzel family and that he felt the situation required Ed and Lorraine's attention. Then he brought them up-to-date on what he'd already done.

Lorraine told Father Dennis that exactly a week earlier, as she and Ed were driving through Brookfield Center, she had felt a wave of evil emanate from the area. From that moment on, Lorraine said, she was beset with an oppressive foreboding. She told Ed and his assistant Paul Bartz that she feared a dangerous case was coming, and, to the best of her ability, she pinpointed the problem to the town of Brookfield.

Although Ed and Lorraine Warren work as an investigative team, each has a separate field of expertise. Lorraine is a clairvoyant and can discern the presence of spirit forces in an environment. Lorraine Warren is unfailingly accurate in determining the nature of invisible intruders. The clergy have quietly called on her for years to discern the name and number of entities during exorcisms. Sometimes she helps police to find hidden links in otherwise unsolvable crimes, and her husband depends on her skill to confirm if a home is truly haunted.

Ed Warren is not psychically endowed, nor is it a feature of his work. His expertise is in the field of religious demonology—the study of diabolical forces. His task is to determine if a disturbance is being caused by a spirit agency. For him, demonology is not a matter of belief but of provable evidence: "There is an orderly, observable process to spirit manifestations, and when they genuinely occur, I work with Lorraine and the clergy to bring an end to the travail a person or family may be experiencing."

That night, immediately after consulting with Father Dennis on the phone, they called their friend Dr. Anthony Giangrasso and asked him to accompany them to Brookfield to investigate a potential outbreak of phenomena. The doctor agreed to accompany them.

For Ed and Lorraine Warren, this was the beginning of the worst case of their lives.

Chapter XI

It was a hot, steamy night, with fog obscuring the road as the group drove to Brookfield Center. No one talked. For Ed and Lorraine Warren, this was the second significant referral they'd had in the state of Connecticut within a year. The summer before, in August 1979, both the New York and Connecticut state police called on the Warrens to investigate "nefarious" activity in the town of Ridgefield, Connecticut, an affluent village on the New York state border. Profane chants, gunshots, and bizarre music had been coming from the property of a prominent rock-and-roll singer. The Warrens were brought in after a Connecticut police officer had been attacked by a mob wearing black hoods and capes. On the property of the singer's mansion, the Warrens discovered the remains of a ritualistic bonfire, ceremonial stakes, and signs of animal sacrifice, all integral elements of Satanic cult activity. Locals scoffed at the Warrens' findings, until months later, when the same entertainer introduced a new form of music: Satan rock.

As the three neared the Glatzels, Ed broke the silence and mentioned to Dr. Tony, as he called him, that this was the second incident to occur in Brookfield that month. Half a dozen people had reported picking up a good looking, well dressed hitchiker along Route 25, but just as soon as the rider got in the car he launched into a diatribe about how the Bible must be read, and how man was "periously close to destroying the earth God gave him". After the hitchiker went through his rap, the driver would discover that his opinionated rider had suddenly disappeared—although his seat belt was still snapped closed.

At 11:30 P.M. they arrived at the Glatzel house. The property was dark and foreboding. Ed led the way up the steep concrete steps to the front door, then unaccountably tripped and fell painfully. Lorraine followed without incident, but halfway up the same steps, Dr. Giangrasso also tripped. As they approached the front door, a person mysteriously came toward them out of the darkness.

"They're all crazy in there," a male voice said. "There's nothing happening. It's all being made up. You ought to go home." It was young Carl.

Ed, as he knocked on the front door, told the young man in the shadows that he'd like to hear the other side of the story before making a decision.

Judy opened the door with the words, "Thank God you're here!"

Inside, the Warrens and Dr. Giangrasso sat at the kitchen table with Judy, David, Arne, Debbie, and Pat Giddings. Alan sat nearby on a stool, while young Carl, who'd entered through the basement, now and then peeked at the strangers from the living room. Curiously absent, the Warrens felt, was the father. Carl had retired an hour earlier, wanting no part of their "crazy problem." Though Carl wouldn't admit it to anyone for some time, that crazy problem became a vivid reality to him that night.

Ed Warren set up a tape-recorder and asked everyone to state their name, address, and age. To keep a record of the case, Ed then had Judy explain the story from the beginning, while the others were to fill in details that she might omit.

Judy started with the situation in the rental house on July 2 and described the events from that day on. The Warrens were listening not just to get a narration of events. They were assessing the credibility of the story, while observing the psychological behavior of the individuals. Was their explanation consistent, or did it change with retelling? Was the language straightforward, or was it full of subjective "I felt" qualifications? Were details exaggerated? Was there a sophisticated knowledge of the occult imbedded in their discourse? Was the story original, or was it the plot of a recent television show?

As Judy continued, the Warrens searched for more significant clues. Was this purely a visionary experience, or were there external factors to corroborate her statements? Since virtually all the people at the table could ratify the existence of external phenomena, it was not an individual psychological problem. Nevertheless, to explore the possibility of a medical and/or psychological factor, Dr. Giangrasso examined David in the living room.

Dr. Anthony Giangrasso, age fifty, is an established physician and a medical examiner for the county. Ed Warren had every confidence that if there was anything wrong with David, the doctor would not only discover it but offer cures as well.

But it was as psychic investigators that the Warrens were present in the Glatzel home. The Warrens knew that if spirit forces were behind the problem, the activity would have developed in a specific, sequential manner. To make a proper determination, the Warrens needed more than a belief in what Judy Glatzel was telling them. "After all," as Lorraine Warren puts it, "people believe lots of things that aren't true." So the Warrens were seeking evidence to substantiate the existence of an intelligence behind the events. If a causal intelligence was at work, a pattern would emerge. The next task would be to discern the nature of that intelligence—human or inhuman.

Having spent their entire adult lives working in this area, the Warrens long ago learned that when spirits are responsible for a disturbance, those spirits are not always human.

"When a spirit intelligence is producing phenomena in a home, it's usually caused by a ghost—the lingering spirit of a human being," says Lorraine Warren. "The ghost syndrome is caused when an individual dies a sudden or traumatic death and is stuck in a state of unresolve. To make the world aware of its presence, the ghost of a deceased person will sometimes manifest, or manipulate the physical environment to call attention to its in-between plight. The ghost wants help, and Ed and I have assisted hundreds of unresolved human spirits to pass on to the next dimension. While active, the phenomena caused by human spirits are random, and very rarely involve the movement of objects. The motive of the entity is to get out of its unhappy predicament, not to provoke fear and scare help away."

"While the human spirit is a lone, individual, unhappy entity with virtually no power to affect the material environment," Ed adds, "there's another type of spirit intelligence one encounters in this work. It is the *inhuman* spirit—an entity so unworthy of life that it has forever been prevented from taking on physical existence. This is the demonic, so called because of its immense, eternal hate of both man and God. The inhuman demonic spirit is a being of another order. It is dedicated to death and ruination. As an entity, the demonic has the power to manipulate the physical environment and can cause enormous damage and destruction. The phenomena caused by the inhuman spirit take place in a deliberate, stagelike manner that is always designed to result in fear, injury, and, where possible, death."

When Judy finished, Debbie gave her own account of the incidents that had occurred, right up to an hour before, when her son, Jason, was pushed head first off the top bunk. Arne then told of the sheepdog's harrowing night in the rental house; the sounds in the Glatzel attic; his mother's drastic change in attitude; and something none of them knew—that during the week, at a neighbor's house, he had been physically picked up and *thrown down the front steps* by an invisible being.

"Everything was usually so quiet over here," Pat Giddings added. "Everyone got along well. Then suddenly it blew up."

"Has David spoken in any voice other than his own?" Ed asked.

"Not that I've heard," Judy replied. "Why?"

"No reason, just curious," Ed said, trying to play down the question.

"Just a minute," Debbie cut in. "David talks in his own speaking voice, but the language he uses isn't his own. He's in a special reading class at school and he talks in a very basic way. When this thing came into the house, David began saying—or rather repeating—words that even he doesn't understand. He'll say *encounter* instead of *meet*, or *agitate* instead of *get upset*. And he curses, too. David never said a dirty word in his life, but when we ask him what the thing said back to us, his answers are full of four-letter words."

Lorraine turned to Judy. "You said you've observed a marked change in two of your sons. What about Alan?"

"Alan's fine," Judy answered, looking at him. "But David, since that first day, has been moody and grumpy and constantly frightened. And my oldest boy, Carl," she went on in desperation, "has said things to me that have broken my heart, and is suddenly using terrible foul language. I've watched that boy change in front of my eyes. Nothing is normal about either of them."

"What's normal for them?" Ed asked.

"Before all this started, Carl was courteous, even-tempered, and calm. I could depend on him. Now I actually think he hates me! And David—he's been a good kid. He'll play for hours, come in and have a glass of milk, then run out and play some more. If you need him to help you, he'll work with you till you're done. But now, well . . . everything's changed," Judy trailed off.

"Does activity go on twenty-four hours a day?" Ed asked.

"Ninety percent of it goes on at night," Judy replied. "It gets really bad after the sun goes down, and gets even more intense in the deep night and early morning hours. Then, before the sun comes up, it starts to wind down. By dawn it's over." The answer was meaningful to Ed.

When Dr. Tony and David returned to the kitchen, the doctor reported that David was physically and mentally stable, noting, however, that he was showing signs of obesity.

After ascertaining that David was feeling fine now, Ed began to question him.

"Back in the beginning, David, I understand you were pushed onto a waterbed. Were you actually pushed, or was that the only way you could describe it?"

"I got pushed. I felt two hands pressing flat on my stomach, then all of a sudden I was pushed backwards, hard."

"Now tell me more about this man," said Ed. "Does his face have eyes and a nose and a mouth and ears?"

"Yeah, all that."

"Does he have arms and legs?"

"Yes."

"Hands and feet?"

"He's got twisty old man's hands, but no, he don't have people feet. They're pointy, like an animal's."

"Pointy feet? You mean cloven?" asked Lorraine.

David didn't understand the word. Judy explained, "Deer's feet, honey."

"That's what he's got, deer's feet," David answered.

Lorraine asked, "David, when did this old man start talking to you?"

"The first day, when I was pushed down, he talked. He pointed right at me and said, 'Beware!'"

"*Beware?* Are you sure of that?" Ed asked.

"I'm sure."

"Now tell me this," Ed continued. "What's the difference between this old man and the figure that comes to you in the night?"

"They're the same, but they look different."

"How do you know that?"

"Because I seen him change. At night he has horns,

not too long, that go straight up, then curve a little at the end. He has big round black eyes. High cheekbones. Ears close to the head with a bit of a point. A black mustache and beard. A white face with red skin. He still has the same deer's feet, but at night he gets a tail behind him, just like the others."

"And how many others are there?"

"Forty-three, including the beast."

"How do you know that's how many there are?"

"Because the leader, the beast, calls each of them by number."

"Don't they have names?"

"I don't know," David said honestly. "I never heard none."

"What do they do when they get near you?" Lorraine asked.

"They all stand around me in a circle and scream at me, and curse at me *all night long*."

"And where did you get the name 'the beast'?" she asked.

"That's the name we gave it," Debbie cut in, "because the only thing it does is act like an animal."

The Warrens were impressed with David. He spoke with great cogency, and his replies were stunningly consistent with their own knowledge of demonic phenomena.

If all proved to be true, there was extraordinary danger in the Glatzel house. Therefore, it was with a sense of urgency that the Warrens decided to challenge the entity called the beast to make its presence known.

"David," Ed said, "you say this thing you call the beast has something like forty others with it. Where are they right now?"

"Most of them are upstairs in the attic, in the rafters, where it's hot. They like the hot. His two main helpers are outside in front. They tripped you and Dr. Tony when you came up the steps."

"How do you know that?" Ed asked quickly.

"The beast told me," David answered, nonplussed.

"And where's the beast now?" Ed asked.

"In the living room, sitting in the rocking chair. The rocking chair is his, he says."

"How do you know the beast is in there?" Lorraine asked. David's back was to the living room and the door was closed.

"Because since they came I can see through walls."

"You can see *through walls?*"

"I couldn't at first, but now I can all the time."

"What's he doing in the living room?" Ed asked.

"He's listening to what we're saying. He doesn't like you. He doesn't want you here."

"I'm sure he doesn't. But if he's so interested, ask him to come into the kitchen with us. That way he can hear better." Ed paused for a moment. "Is he here?"

"There's *something* here," Lorraine announced in a hushed voice. "It's standing next to David."

"Is that true, David?" Ed asked.

David, glancing slightly to his right said, "Yeah, he's right next to me."

"What does it look like, Lorraine?" Ed asked.

"It's not showing with features," she said. "But there's a very distinct spirit mass, gray black, six feet tall, on the child's right."

"I wonder if he'd like to have his picture taken, since he's so bold," Ed said.

"He says, don't you dare," David reported.

"Why, is he afraid?"

"Not of you, he says."

"I think he's afraid for people to know he exists."

111

"He says, how'd you like to be thrown out the window?"

"Yes. I'd like that very much. But I don't think he could do it though."

"He says he will."

"When is he going to do this?" Ed asked, continuing the challenge.

"In about ten seconds, he says, if you don't shut up."

"I don't think he has the power!"

"He says, if he had the power to throw Arne down the steps, he has the power to throw you out of his house."

"*His* house? Tell him I said God is more powerful than he could ever be."

"He says, no He isn't!"

"Well, if He isn't, then I should be out the window by now. I think he can only strangle little boys and stick magic knives in them."

"He says, go to hell!"

"Tell him when I bring priests in here, that's just where he's going."

"Never, he says. No Goddamn priest will ever drive him out. He'll drive every priest away you try to bring in here!"

"We'll see about that," Ed replied. "Tell me, what does he call himself? He must have a name. What's his name?"

"He says, his name is Satan."

Judy Glatzel gasped.

"Satan, huh? Well, Satan, if you're so powerful and you haven't been able to throw me out the window, then how do I really know you're here?"

Suddenly it felt like the whole floor had been hit from below.

112

"Very impressive, Satan," Ed told the force. Worried that the tape-recorder might not have picked up the sound, he goaded the beast: "But I'd like you to knock three times on the table, just so I can be certain there's no mistake."

There was a long pause; then, loudly enough to give goosebumps to everyone, three knocks sounded on the table. It was clearly loud enough to be picked up on the tape-recorder.

If an intelligence was indeed behind the phenomena, then it could be provoked to repeat the activity. Hence, Ed Warren deliberately provoked the force by saying, "You know, Satan, I've heard ghosts do better than that. Do it again."

"He says, he's not taking orders from you," David reported.

"Oh really? I don't think he *can* do it again. I think he's just a ghost. I think he just used every bit of energy he had to rap on the table. I think it'll take him a whole day to store up enough power to do it again."

Three forceful thumps hit the floor, followed by more knocking on the table.

"If you can do all that, Satan, then how about showing yourself to us right here, right now?"

"He said something dirty," David reported.

"Well, if you don't show yourself, Satan, then how can I know you're not just a ghost?"

More knocking sounds were heard.

After a long pause, David said, "He's laughing at you. He says, you ask foolish questions."

"What's foolish about asking if he's a ghost?"

"He says, *you know why!* He says, there's a big difference, and he's no Goddamn man!"

"Oh, there's a difference, is there?" Ed said knowingly. "And what would that difference be?"

"You're making him mad," David remarked. "He says you talk to him like a fool, but we're the ones who are all stupid."

"We're stupid?"

"He says, the difference between him and man is that a ghost has a soul."

"Doesn't he have a soul?"

"No. He says, *he has no soul!*"

The Warrens terminated the interrogation. After two hours of hard questioning, they had a good initial understanding of the case and were satisfied that there was substance to the story.

The Warrens found the Glatzels to be sincere, credible people of sound mind and character. Their psychological behavior was normal; drugs or alcohol did not appear to be a factor; a physician's examination of David failed to turn up any medical explanation for the phenomena.

The Glatzels' detailed story was corroborated at every key point. The activity they described was consistent with the known workings of spirit phenomena.

An intelligence had shown itself to be behind the disturbance. At least one entity had been discerned, and that entity had been provoked to produce externalized phenomena, that were perceived by the human senses and were recorded for later substantiation.

The nature of the entity's intelligence had been revealed as nonhuman. Clearly, this wasn't a ghost. If a spirit entity was responsible for the disturbance, it was a serious one, and potentially demonic. Therefore, the Warrens endorsed Father Dennis's recommendation of prayer and the reading of psalms as the proper response to any further outbreak of activity.

The Warrens also recommended that one member of the family begin keeping a journal of events, should it become necessary to document the progression of the case.

Having done all they could, the Warrens left the Glatzel home with Dr. Giangrasso at approximately one-thirty in the morning, promising to return the next evening.

But as soon as the Warrens arrived at their home in Monroe, the Glatzels called them. They were under attack! Ed and Lorraine Warren immediately rushed back to Brookfield.

The reason for their urgent return is evident in the pages of Debbie Glatzel's journal for July 14, 1980:

At 1:50 A.M.: In the kitchen, David, standing, got stabbed in the front and back near the heart. I touched him with holy water and made the sign of the cross. Cheyenne read Psalm 23.

At 2:30 A.M.: In the kitchen, David, sitting in the chair, began to get stomach pains, severe, and was going to start throwing up, but I stopped him with holy water, made the sign of the cross on his throat, and Chey read Psalm 23.

At 4:21 A.M.: David got shot with a handgun [revolver] in the stomach. I made the sign of the cross and Chey read Psalm 23.

The spirits told David he'd be sorry if the Warrens came. He was.

Chapter XII

Having interviewed the Glatzels and later having witnessed David Glatzel under attack during the early morning hours of July 14, the Warrens had little doubt that what was happening in Brookfield conformed to the known stages of preternatural manifestation.

Demonology is a category of theology, and as an academic discipline it has its own literature and history of cases that have been studied extensively over the years. The subject is taught only in seminaries, and the pontifical universities in Rome.

In January 1975, however, a closed-door, invitation-only conference was held in the United States, at the University of Notre Dame. The conference, "A Theological, Psychological, Medical Symposium on the Phenomenon Labeled as Demonic," resulted in the presentation of some twenty-four scholarly papers,* which

---

*These papers resulted in a book, *Demon Possession*, John Warwick Montgomery (ed.), Minneapolis: Bethany Fellowship, 1976.

confirmed the austere reality of diabolical oppression and possession.

Preternatural manifestations occur in a five-step progression: encroachment, infestation, oppression, possession, and death. Demonologist Ed Warren explains:

"First occurs the encroachment—or permission—stage, where a negative spirit is given access to a human being through either voluntary means (satanic rituals) or involuntary means (curses). The essential point to remember is that doors have to be opened for the phenomena to occur. Leave the occult alone and your chances of having spirit problems is almost nil.

"Next comes the infestation stage, where negative spirits physically enter the homes or lives of human beings and cause fearful phenomena. For some strange reason the infesting entity presents itself only after making an obvious, comprehensible warning of its arrival, such as three audible knocks at the door.

"If it is not stopped or recognized, activity will intensify up to the oppression (or obsession) stage, where the infesting entity seeks to overwhelm and subdue the will of the person being possessed. Oppression takes two forms, which can occur simultaneously. External oppression is the daunting of the human intellect through manipulation of the physical environment, resulting in wholesale terror; internal oppression is the interference or manipulation of thoughts and emotions, resulting in the modification of behavior or the triggering of inappropriate responses to ordinary events. During oppression, the entity's objective is complete dominance of the human will, through either terror or capitulation. Once in charge, the entity will either oppress the individual to the point where he tries to kill himself or others, or it will proceed to the next stage.

118

"The fourth stage—and the objective of all the activity that preceded it—is the diabolical possession of a human being. This is the triumph of the inhuman entity. From its seat in the person, the negative spirit tyrannizes the physical body it has stolen, and proceeds to impose its will on the people around it. When possession occurs, the human spirit is displaced from the body and replaced by an inhuman spirit. As the inhuman spirit is unworthy of life, and named in the Gospels as 'a murderer from the very beginning,' tragedy is the only predictable outcome of possession.

"The fifth and final step in the progression is death. Starting with a perhaps unnoticed encroachment and working through the stages from infestation to oppression to possession, the infernal plan—if not stopped— may result in death. As a spirit of perdition, the inhuman entity seeks to bring about suicide, murder, or both."

When the Warrens reviewed the tapes they'd made the night before at the Glatzel house, they confirmed that this sequence was under way.

Encroachment appeared to have resulted from interactions with negative spirit forces inside the rental house in Newtown. Why it had picked on David and young Carl was yet to be learned.

Infestation had certainly occurred. The so-called beast had first given the mandatory warning: *Beware!* It had also made itself visible to David the very first day—a bad sign. "The weaker the entity," notes Ed Warren, "the more it depends on invisibility; the stronger the entity, the bolder it behaves. In half the cases we investigate, the afflicted individuals never see what is tormenting them. The knockings and other sounds were also infestation phenomena, designed simply to scare the victims."

Oppression, the third stage of the sinister progression, had definitely been reached. Both internal and external oppression phenomena were now occurring. Gruesome entities were routinely showing themselves to the child, intimidating him not just psychologically but with physical violence. Material objects were being levitated, thrown, or moved about in the house; even people were being picked up and tossed around. There had also been drastic mood changes and violent arguments among the formerly close family members.

What troubled the Warrens most, however, was the swiftness of the progression and the intensity of the oppression phenomena. In many cases they'd investigated, the movement from one stage to the next took weeks, months, or sometimes years. Here, the progression happened in a matter of days. The oppression phenomena were not just intimidating but downright violent. The power of the activity far exceeded any understandable function.

As the Warrens neared the end of the tape, it became evident that David was already exhibiting what seemed to be signs of transient possession! He could see through walls; he could accurately describe activity taking place at a distance; and his uncanny predictions indicated sudden precognition. This represented the intercession of a more powerful, overlording force in the child's immediate life, and the Warrens suspected that something was speaking through David, or at least filling his mind with information that he would not ordinarily have known.

Now the Warrens' most pressing concern was to uncover the source of the initial encroachment. Knowing how the case started might enable them to stop the process.

The second interview with the Glatzels, on the afternoon of July 14, disproved the theory that the initial encroachment, or permission for the spirits' entry into their lives, had occurred on July 2 at the rental house. Instead, the Warrens learned, the Glatzels, like a great many other Americans, had dabbled in the occult.

In the early 1970s, a course on witchcraft and the occult was offered at Brookfield High School. At that time, there was enormous interest in astrology and the supernatural. Debbie Glatzel took the course as an elective, and wrote a short paper on witchcraft. This heightened her interest in the occult, and when she graduated, she went a step further and bought a Ouija board.

Like most people who've never played with the board, she considered it a toy. She didn't know the Ouija board could be, as the Warrens put it, "a telegraph set to the beyond." Unfortunately, she was one of the few people who got the board to really work.

"It was talkative," Debbie told Ed and Lorraine Warren. "When I used it with someone, usually my mother, Alan, or a girl friend, it gave true answers. The thing was really prissy, though; it said it wouldn't talk to me unless I kept it spotlessly dusted and stored it in a pillowcase under my bed. It said it liked the dark. One time it even said it wanted me to 'make love' to it, however you were supposed to do that."

"That would have been an Incubus entity," Lorraine replied, "a spirit of lust. Did it give a name?"

"Yes, it gave me a weird name, full of z's and k's, but I couldn't pronounce it," Debbie answered. "The thing said it had died in a dungeon for something it didn't do."

"Did it tell you anything of substance, or was it just a lot of nonsense?" Ed asked.

"There was no nonsense about it. One night, when

I was pregnant, I asked if I'd have a boy or a girl. It said a boy. I kept asking questions, and it told me the month, day, and minute of the child's birth, and it's exact weight, *to the ounce!* When Jason was born, every prediction it had given me proved to be absolutely true!"

"What became of the board?" Lorraine asked.

"It became so real it scared me, and I threw it out. I just knew there was something wrong about it: the thing seemed to have a mind of its own."

"You said you wrote a witchcraft paper. Did you ever perform any kind of ritual or incantation?" Ed asked.

"No. It wasn't that kind of paper—it was historical."

"How does all this relate to David?" Judy asked the Warrens.

"Use of the Ouija board was more than a means of communication, I'm afraid," Lorraine explained. "The act of using the board worked as a form of permission for spirits to come into your life."

"Then that thing in the board years ago is attacking David now?" Judy questioned.

"No, not necessarily," Lorraine replied. "But it did unlock the door to your inner selves. It's been unlocked all this time. Sooner or later something was bound to walk in. It made you vulnerable. We call it the Law of Invitation. A dozen people may have been able to live in that rental house without any problem, but because you were vulnerable, whatever spirit forces were there had access to you. You know you were victims because you experienced outward phenomena; other people just get their lives ruined and never know why."

The Warrens were at the Glatzel house that afternoon to determine the origin of the case. But rather than narrowing down the problem, the situation became more complex. The Warrens learned that the beast and its forty-two helpers virtually commuted between Brookfield and the rental house, and that the beast had taken a shine to Carl Glatzel, Sr., who lacked the protection of baptism. Unknown to many, baptism is a combined ritual of exorcism and dedication of the new infant spirit to God, ostensibly providing a protection against evil man is not born with. The Warrens also found out that David was four years late in making his First Holy Communion; that Carl Jr., had an aversion to religion; and that Arne and Debbie were living as man and wife but had not yet gotten married. But the biggest question was why David and Carl, Jr., had been singled out for oppression and attack. They seemed only innocent pawns in a much larger game. Tragically, the reason for their oppression proved to be one of the best-kept secrets of the case.

Before leaving, Ed Warren wanted to see David, who was holed up in his bedroom. Ed found David sitting on the floor, leafing through comic books.

David didn't even look up when the door was opened. He turned a couple of pages, and then in an uncharacteristically snide manner remarked, "Well well, if it ain't the big demonologist!"

Ed Warren was surprised. He had never mentioned his work to anyone in the family. "How do you know that?" he asked.

David stared contemptuously at him. "Buzz off, creep!"

"I thought I could just talk to you for a minute, David," Ed pressed. But that was it. David refused to answer, and ignored Ed until he left.

David was in a wicked quandary. He truly wanted help, but he dared not take it. The beast threatened the child continuously, and for cooperating with Father Dennis and the Warrens, he was beaten and tortured.

The Warrens left an hour after arriving, but insisted that Judy call them immediately if there was any trouble. And indeed there was.

That night, just after nine o'clock, David was "shot" in the head by the beast for being "recalcitrant" about getting holy objects out of his bedroom, and as punishment for the Warrens' second visit.

But it was at ten-forty that the situation became really grave, and Judy, desperate, called the Warrens.

It started as David was watching television with Arne, Debbie, and Alan. Suddenly David's arms and legs began to quiver uncontrollably.

"Help!" David cried out.

The family watched in horror as David's eyeballs rolled slowly up into his head. All that could be seen were the whites of his eyes. A strange groaning noise then emanated from David's body.

"Arne, get the holy water, quick!" Debbie urged, never looking away from her brother.

As Arne returned to the living room, David's eyeballs very slowly came back down. However, now his pupils were fully dilated. David seemed different, and beamed a ray of hatred in Arne's direction, stopping him dead in his tracks.

"Hit him with the holy water!" Debbie shouted.

"Keep that foul piss away from me!" David responded, in a voice that sounded more like an evil parody than the voice of a child.

All were frozen in place as David sat like a fat, vulgar, little boy-king commanding his elders, a sneer of hatred contorting his face.

"Come near me, Johnson," he proclaimed in his adulterated voice, "and I'll kill you!"

"Don't talk like that, David," said Arne, hurt and perplexed.

"Fuck you, fucker!" was the little boy's gross reply.

"Hit him with it, Arne!" Debbie insisted.

"All right, buddy, I'm coming." Arne took a step forward.

David's mouth dropped open and emitted a vicious, animal growl.

David Glatzel, even in his most active moments, moves slowly at best, but before Arne could take a second step toward him, David sprang off the couch and wrapped his arm around his brother Alan's neck. Then David reached into his pocket and produced a pen knife, which he dexterously opened with one hand, and placed the short, sharp blade against Alan's neck.

"Throw that piss water on me and I'll kill this little bastard right now," David warned in his spurious voice. "*I hate you!* I hate you *all!* Do you you hear me? I'll kill him right now! *Get away from me!*"

Arne backed off and put the holy water on a nearby table.

David's eyes darted around the room and fixed on the front door. "I'll kill anybody who gets in my way!" he shouted, bolting across the room to the door. He dropped the knife and in a flash snapped back the locks and opened the door.

But Arne was quicker. He grabbed David by the shoulders, hauled him back inside, and knocked him backward onto the couch.

David lay on his back like a cornered animal. Arne was afraid to get too close.

"What do you think you're doing?" Arne asked. "How could you talk like that?" In response, David snarled.

"Get the Bible, Debbie, and hand me the holy water," Arne said, disgusted.

Immediately, David screamed and jumped up, his face contorted with loathing. As Arne came toward him, David spat in his face, then tried to run to the kitchen. Debbie tackled him. David pulled her down to the floor and wrestled with her until Arne was able to separate them. By now Arne had had enough. He grabbed David by the front of his shirt and in one motion swung him in an arc across the room and onto the couch.

When Arne cast holy water at David and blessed him with the sign of the cross, David suddenly flew at Arne, grasping him around the neck with both hands in a genuine effort to kill him. Debbie helped force David's hands off Arne's neck, but then David got loose again, growling as he demanded that they keep away from him.

Finally, with Alan's help, they got David onto the couch again, where he flopped over on his back, panting and exhausted.

Arne began reading Psalm 23 " 'The Lord is my shepherd; I shall not want. He maketh me to lie down in green pastures; he . . .' "

The Lord is a dipshit," said the man-child voice in David.

" '. . . He leadeth me beside the still waters. He restoreth my soul: He . . .' "

God will not help you. This soul is mine!" The words were followed by raucous laughter.

" '. . . He leadeth me in the paths of righteousness for his name's sake. Yea, though I walk through the valley of the shadow of death, I will fear no evil: for thou art . . .' "

"Look!" Debbie cried.

David's stomach was beginning to swell. It balooned

until his whole abdominal region was double its normal size.

There was nothing they could do to stop the grotesque distortion. Finally, by the time Arne had read the psalm twice, David's stomach began slowly to deflate to near normal size. But it wasn't over: David had stopped breathing and was turning blue from lack of oxygen.

Debbie slapped his face, shook him, and performed artificial respiration. But David didn't respond.

Arne desperately began pressing and releasing David's chest. But still there was no response. At her wit's end, Debbie blessed her brother's forehead with holy water, begging for God's help, while Arne kept working feverishly. "I . . . I think maybe he's dead," Arne whispered.

"Call for an ambulance, mom!" Debbie shouted. "Hurry!"

Judy had already dialed the operator when David began moaning softly, then wearily opened his eyes and drew a deep breath. He was soon back to normal.

Curiously, the attack stopped the moment the Warrens pulled into the driveway. Ed and Lorraine Warren, Dr. Giangrasso, and Ed's assistant, John Kenyhercz, rushed into the house barely a minute after the assault had ended. David lay on the couch dripping with sweat and physically drained.

"You won't believe what we've been through!" Judy said. She then described what had just happened. "I hate to say this . . . I don't want to say it . . . but I think David was *possessed*."

Ed looked at the otherwise normal child now sitting up on the couch, then turned to Judy and replied, "No, that's out of the question. Something may have been talking through him; something may have attacked him from outside his body; but if David was truly possessed, you wouldn't think it—you'd know it."

Chapter XIII

Early in the morning of July 15, the Warrens left the Glatzel house convinced that something official had to be done to prevent the very dangerous situation from escalating into a diabolical seige, or even worse, possession.

Wisely, they did not discuss their fears with the family. Instead, they conferred with Father Dennis in Brookfield. In the Warrens' professional judgment, exorcism of the premises was necessary.

Father Dennis had reluctantly come to the same conclusion. Caution had been the initial watchword in the Glatzel case, but now it appeared there was no alternative to the solemn procedure of exorcism.

Although no one in the Glatzel family was told of the Warrens' decisive conversation with Father Dennis, spirit activity in the Glatzel home unexpectedly and inexplicably stopped. David reported that the beast and its helpers had withdrawn to the rental house in Newtown and stayed there.

"Did the thing tell you why it left?" Judy asked.

"He just said we're too much trouble," David answered.

The following day, when Father Dennis came to see the Glatzels, expecting that exorcism of the premises would have to be recommended to the diocese, he was relieved to learn there was nothing *to* expel. Nevertheless, he warned the family to remain vigilant—to keep the holy candles lit, and not to stop praying. To strengthen David, he left books to help the boy to prepare for making his First Holy Communion that summer. As further defense, he gave David a holy relic of St. John Bosco, a saint whose life had been dedicated to the education of children.

Beginning on July 15, peace reigned in the Glatzel home. The invasion seemed over, and everyone concerned was enormously relieved.

Arne and Debbie, however, feared that the beast might only have directed its energies elsewhere—specifically, to his mother and the girls. On Sunday, he and Debbie drove to the rental house in Newtown.

The visit was not a pleasant one. Mary Johnson was uncharacteristically bitter and hostile. She rejected any suggestion of supernatural danger in the house.

Although Mary and the girls had not experienced any real crisis, life at the rental house was hardly normal. With the owner's daughter still occupying the attached apartment, the girls complained that they were forbidden to go into the garage, the locked storage room, the backyard, and the front yard. In addition, their dog, Pepper, was not allowed to run loose; and the girls were accused of trying to cause flat tires by throwing twigs in the driveway.

Inside the house, matters were similarly disturbing, especially for the two youngest girls—Mary, nine, and

Jannie, twelve. They were "afraid" in the house. In the middle of the night they heard knocks on the doors and taps on the windows. Pepper whined all night and frequently barked and growled at the basement door for no understandable reason. Previously healthy houseplants wilted and died. The two little girls finally admitted that they slept on the floor in their mother's room. But Wanda, the eldest, like Carl, Jr., heard nothing, saw nothing, and felt nothing. She comfortably occupied a bedroom of her own and told the other two girls they were "crazy" and "making things up." Mary Johnson supported Wanda, leaving the two youngest girls even more upset.

But Arne's mother couldn't deny the curious incident she witnessed that afternoon. Mrs. Johnson wouldn't go into the basement alone, and had waited a week for someone to accompany her downstairs to retrieve some boxes. Even Arne was reluctant to go into the cellar, but he thought it might appease his mother if he complied. After Mary had gotten what she needed, Arne walked up the stairs ahead of her. When Arne was halfway up, he felt an ice-cold hand grasp one of his ankles. A moment later, the hand yanked his foot off the step, causing him to fall down the stairs.

Arne's mother Mary was appalled. "Something grabbed your ankle!" she said, incredulous.

"I know," Arne replied dryly.

Arne and Debbie's trip to the Newtown house was a bittersweet affair: his sisters wanted them to come back and live with them, but Arne's mother did not. When Arne and Debbie left the house, it was like people looking through a fence: they were a family divided by a barrier that none of them wanted to be there.

Meanwhile, all remained quiet in the Glatzel home.

By Friday, July 25, the family was sure the terrible ordeal was a thing of the past.

Little did they know that all the while they were being watched, and that the beast was actually waiting to take David into mortal bondage.

The first sign was an innocuous one. Lying in his bed that Friday night, David heard a young girl calling to him from a distance: "Daaaaaviiiiiid . . . Help me . . . Help me, Daaaviiid . . ."

The voice David heard wasn't frightening, just unsettling. But he refused to pay any attention to it, and he slept well that night.

But something happened to Alan the following day. He was alone in the house, sitting at the kitchen table playing solitaire. All was quiet. Suddenly from the master bedroom came the distinct sound of a hissing snake—a big snake; a cobra, Alan called it. Shortly thereafter, he heard whisperings in the hallway. The words were undecipherable, but the sense of a presence was sufficiently real to terrify the boy. When Judy, David, Jason, and young Carl returned from a few hours at the town beach, they found Alan in tears.

Next, big, fat flies began to appear in the house. They congregated on the insides of the windows and in the corners of ceilings. When attacked with bug spray, they swirled to the floor and merely disappeared. When hit with a flyswatter, they lay inert for a moment, then flew again. The flies could not have come from outside, because the house was filtered by air-conditioning and the windows were kept closed.

David later explained that these unusually large flies were the "bugs" released by the beast when it had first opened the black box. David had "seen" the flies all along, swirling among the multitude of helpers, but now they were flying in the physical dimension as well.

Disturbed by these incidents, Judy called the Warrens. They explained that such whisperings usually were heard at the very beginning or the very end of a case. Their function was to arouse fear. Ed Warren told her to recite a prayer in the hallway to neutralize the force, and to instruct the others to ignore the phenomenon lest it get a foothold again. The Warrens did not know why the activity had started again.

Much later, it became apparent that Father Dennis posed a threat to the invading entities. The priest had every intention of recommending that the entities be expelled permanently by exorcism. Evidently the entities knew this, and they did not manifest again—at least not until the night of Sunday, July 27. On that night, Father Dennis departed for Ireland.

Father Dennis called the Warrens that Sunday afternoon and told them he'd be gone until September. If there was any more difficulty, the assistant pastor, Father James Grosso, would be arriving back from vacation in a few days to take charge of the parish in his absence. In the meantime, a newly ordained priest, Father William Millea, was in charge. Fathers Grosso and Millea were aware of the case in Brookfield, but if problems developed, the Warrens would have to brief them on relevant details.

No sooner was Father Dennis airborne than problems erupted in the Glatzel house. This time, however, even Carl Glatzel took heed. As the family sat around the dinner table that night, a freshly made chocolate cake eerily rose off the counter and pressed into the bottom of a kitchen cabinet, smearing icing all over the woodwork before sinking back down again, ruined.

Later that evening Judy's makeup case rose off a table and hit David in the chest. As soon as it was picked up and returned to the table, the case flew

133

again, this time hitting David in the ear. Debbie then took the makeup case into the bathroom, but it promptly came whizzing out again and hit David a third time.

Arne was about to pick up the case and return it to the bathroom when he suddenly saw a specter in gray surrounded with a black outline. It was roughly the size and shape of a man, but without any specific features, except two large, dark "eyes" staring out at him. The thing was not human. When Arne turned to call Debbie, the thing disappeared.

Later that same night, at 1:45 A.M., the family was awakened by what sounded like an explosion in David and Alan's room. By the time Carl and Judy ran into the room, an intense whirring vibration had started near Alan's bed. It was the same sound David had heard the first time the beast had manifested itself to him.

The humming soon moved into the center of the room. Alan said he was going to tape the noise, and turned on his cassette recorder.

"That won't run," David said.

Alan was frustrated to find that his brother was correct: the machine wouldn't work.

The humming stopped near the foot of David's bed. Everyone's ears rang from the sound. The noise faded, but David sat staring intently ahead of him.

"What do you see?" Alan asked.

David was silent for a few moments, then answered, "There's a strong blue ball of light by me that's getting bigger." Edging back in the bed while staring open-mouthed, David then said, "It's him! He's coming. . . ."

All stood transfixed at the scene.

"David, please, what is it?" Judy begged.

Slowly the boy turned his head and looked at her

with sneering derision. The eyes did not blink; the mouth did not open. *"His soul,"* an alien voice declared, *"is mine!"*

Judy called Ed Warren the next morning. "The beast came back last night and took him over. It said, now that Father Dennis is out of the way, it's taking charge. No one—not you, not a priest, not even God—is going to stop it." Judy then gave the phone to David.

"He said he's come to stay and he's gonna take a soul, and he don't care whose," David declared. "He says, you wait, we'll all be sorry. Anyone who comes here, even the priests, is gonna get beaten down or tormented away. He says, no one is gonna be able to help. He'll make everyone turn against us—even the Church. He's gonna make us look like fools and liars. He'll make everyone betray everyone else. And there's gonna be *death*. Nothing will work, and a year from now he'll still be here—only things'll be worse!"

"Who did he say is going to die?" Ed asked.

"He'll tell us when the time comes, he said."

Though no one knew it, David had laid out the unfortunate scenario that would come to pass.

That night, after two weeks of calm and quiet, David was again attacked. As in the beginning, when David was slapped or punched, the sound could be heard and the effects could be seen. But now there was a new intensity to the actions: it appeared as if the beast was *really* trying to kill the boy.

A typical incident occurred the afternoon of Monday, July 28. Judy found David on his back in the living room, fighting desperately to free himself from being violently strangled. Her shrieks stopped the attack, but as soon as David was on his feet, he was punched in the stomach so hard that he doubled over and vomited.

Later that afternoon, David came screaming through the house, then fell face down on the kitchen floor, convulsed with pain. Afterward, he told her the two helpers had been whipping him. When it was over, the boy's back was actually covered with welts.

Judy broke down. She was tired of throwing around holy water like some kind of religious fanatic; she was tired of it all. She couldn't understand what her family had done to deserve this, or why the entities wouldn't go away.

Debbie called St. Joseph's and spoke with Father Millea, who invited them to come to the rectory and talk things over.

After an hour's conversation, the young priest was greatly disturbed by the Glatzels' story. He did all he could to refute their assertion that it was a spirit force causing havoc in their lives. Yet, the two women sounded sincere, and the priest wavered in his thinking.

Judy and Debbie, however, left the rectory feeling the priest did not believe them. They did not know that Father Millea simply needed to buy more time in order to advise them properly.

That night, after reflecting on what the Glatzel women had said, Father Millea called the Warrens. By the time the young priest hung up he was deeply troubled. In fact he didn't even want to sleep alone in the rectory.

He called his friend, Father Steve DiGiovanni, assigned to a parish in nearby Norwalk, and asked if he'd come up and stay with him at St. Joseph's for a few days.

Father DiGiovanni arrived shortly after midnight. Neither knew it at the time, but together they would experience the fury of a devil.

Chapter XIV

For the Glatzel family, the world outside their front door was no help. They were living a real but very private hell. Tears of anguish and frustration replaced all joy in their lives.

Every day David watched his friends playing outside, and he yearned to be with them. But Judy could no longer allow him to go out. He was being attacked night and day, outdoors as well as in. If he wasn't being beaten physically, he was being tormented mentally. Worse, whatever was manipulating the boy moved him to extremes of such hate and fury that he couldn't be trusted alone for even a moment. What looked out through David's eyes was not an innocent child: it was the stern, cold gaze of a killer. Matters had degenerated to the point where Judy refused to be left alone in the house with David—or what remained of him.

By the end of July, diabolical activity in the Glatzel

home was continuous—twenty-four hours a day. The pressure was so unbearable for Judy that on July 30 she again called the rectory; this time, she begged Father Millea to come to the house.

Both Father Millea and Father DiGiovanni visited Judy that afternoon. But no discernible phenomena occurred in their presence. David was not helpful: he escaped from the house and hid as soon as the priests arrived. Judy was left to look like a fool—the modern suburban housewife in her no-wax kitchen, so bored with life that she turned to fabricating ghost stories.

Excusing herself, Judy went on a quick hunt and found David locked inside the station wagon. He looked disturbed and dangerous, but she didn't care. She forcibly brought him inside so the priests could speak with him. But when David laid eyes on the clergymen he went wild and broke away from his mother, screaming, "Get those bastards out of here before I kill them!" David then locked himself in the bathroom and fled through the window.

The shocking behavior gave the priests a first-hand sampling of the problem. It was not the intention of either priest to discredit or deny Judy Glatzel's claims; instead, they were looking for information. Since Father Millea had already questioned Judy at the rectory, it was now Father DiGiovanni's turn.

The young priest began by asking about the family's medical and psychological background. While Father DiGiovanni found nothing noteworthy about the family's psychological history, it was apparent that they had experienced a variety of severe physical injuries. A year and a half earlier, in spring 1979, following a trip to upstate New York, Judy collapsed in the doorway of the kitchen and was bedridden for a month with sciatic-nerve trouble. Strangely, the first day she was back on her feet and able to walk, Carl Glatzel collapsed in the very same spot. Suddenly, he couldn't walk: he, too, was crippled with sciatica. Judy noted also that various members of the family had felt a "cold spot" in that very place in the kitchen ever since the troubles began on July 2.

In 1977, David had been sledding and came into the house with a foot-long stake imbedded in his stomach—an injury so severe that his spleen had to be removed.

Four years earlier, young Carl had fallen off his bike. When Carl, Sr., walked into the hospital emergency room and saw his son's mangled face and broken jaw, he fainted.

— Then Judy made a curious aside. David's injury in 1977 and her and Carl's sciatic-nerve trouble in 1979 happened immediately upon returning from their annual snowmobile trip to Old Forge, New York. There, ever since 1976, they had weekended with the same people, whose name Judy recalled for the priests.

"Were these people into the occult?" Father Millea asked. "Did you hold a seance or something?"

"No," Judy replied, "all we did was snowmobile together."

Father DiGiovanni asked if anyone in the family had been experimenting with the occult during those periods. "Only in 1973," Judy said, "and that was just the Ouija board."

"What was the purpose in using the Ouija board?" Father Millea asked.

"Entertainment," Judy replied. "Everybody's interested in the future."

Next, Father DiGiovanni moved into that area beyond the occult—sin—which causes people to be vulnerable to the diabolic from the religious point of view.

Seeking to hide nothing, Judy made a full confession to the priests in her living room. With certain exceptions, it was obvious that all the Glatzels lived respectable lives. The need for the sacraments was the most outstanding problem: baptism for Carl, Sr.; First Holy Communion for David; confirmation for Carl, Jr.; and matrimony for Arne and Debbie. However, according to the priests, these were not the kinds of things that provoked diabolical intervention of the magnitude they were reportedly experiencing.

"You say this supposed spirit talks to David. What does it say?" Father DiGiovanni asked.

Judy told the priests that the beast made David reveal the sins and deep personal secrets of every member of the house. It was mortifying, she said, to hear David spew woefully accurate details of sexual experiences and private conversations he couldn't possibly know anything about.

"David tells us things that happened before he was even born!" Judy continued. "He gives us full descriptions of relatives he's never seen, even though they're dead. And he not only tells us humiliating things about our past—he tells us what's going to happen today, tonight, and tomorrow. We have no more secrets. And every prediction he makes comes true."

Having provided more than ample background, Judy then described the whole range of phenomena she and her family had seen. Beaten and weary after two nights without sleep, Judy was sincere, and both priests believed her and promised to help. They would now see to it that Father Grosso, who was in charge of the church during Father Dennis's absence, was informed about the case so steps could be taken to end the torment.

In the driveway, the priests had another conversation.

"I bet my mother's been telling you all sorts of lies about a ghost in the house. She's been telling that to everyone. There's nothing happening. I haven't seen or heard one thing happen. I ought to know, I live here," young Carl said. "Even my father doesn't believe her. The only thing that's wrong with David is that he's mentally ill. He always has been. My mother only makes this stuff up so she doesn't have to admit it. She's crazy. I'm the only sane one. Ask anybody."

Fortunately, the two priests saw right through young Carl. Upon returning to the rectory, they informed Father Grosso of the disturbing situation at the Glatzel home. That night, Father Grosso called the Warrens to get their opinion. The Warrens, who'd logged in many long hours with the Glatzels, proposed a meeting.

The next day, July 31, Father Grosso and Father Millea went to the Warrens' home in Monroe. Initially, Father Grosso was skeptical about possession and exorcism and all the "nonsense" about the devil and his naughty doings.

"I grew up in an Italian family, and I've heard every superstition that exists about devils, demons, and hell," Father Grosso told the Warrens, "and none of it has ever been proven to me. People have no more truck with devils than they do with angels. They don't exist on the earthly plane. Never as a priest—never as a person—have I ever witnessed one thing that could even remotely be called preternatural phenomena."

The Warrens are aware that the clergy are often the harshest critics of theological dogma, particularly in areas where it is difficult to distinguish faith from fantasy.

"We've found that to be true with most people. But in this situation, opinions aren't good enough," Ed Warren explained to Father Grosso. "Action on this case is your responsibility. The Glatzel family have trouble of a religious nature. They're going to ask you for help, and when that happens, *you* have to make an informed decision about what to do.

"We're not asking you to take our word for it. In the next day or two you'll have to go into that house and see it all for yourself. Maybe we missed something; maybe you'll call it another way; but the judgment is going to be on your shoulders. We feel you should go in there prepared, along with an open mind: your knowledge and training and common sense will do the rest."

Fortunately, Ed Warren's explanation made sense to Father Grosso. By the time the priests left, they had received a rather intense "tutorial" on demonology. Each took with him a handful of books on the subject to read during the next few days.

What may have been only theory to the priests was a painful reality for the Glatzels. Although it is said that "anonymity is the devil's best protection," what had invaded the Glatzel home now seemed to have lost interest in concealing its presence. Extreme cold was felt wherever the beast was present. A dark form moved at will through the house after sunset. And globes of light and crude spirit forms were now being picked up on Polaroid snapshots.

In the early morning hours of August 1, matters hit an ominous new low.

The beast and its two grotesque helpers were furious about the introduction of the new priests into the case. In response came an ultimatum from the beast, followed by a foreboding prediction. With the forty other entities now assembled in the background for

David to see, the beast demanded that the boy "give up" his soul to them so *they* could be done with the whole affair.

Even as the demands were being made, David spoke back to them, insisting, "No! I won't do that! Get away from me!"

Finally, there was a long silence as David sat listening intently. "What are they telling you, David?" Judy asked, obviously worried.

"All of them were screaming at me for a long time, and then they stopped. After that, all of the helpers were staring at me. The leader said he wanted me to go with him, and I said 'no.' Now he's real mad. I don't know what he's gonna do next. But he said, he ran out of patience and now he's not gonna be kind anymore. He said, he's gonna get my soul and Cheyenne's soul too. Since we won't give up to him, he said, he's gonna take us—or kill us! All our hands are gonna be full. He says, *he's gonna get into our bodies!* And if anybody gets in his way, to stop him, he'll kill them!"

"Nobody's going to get killed!" Arne said angrily, "because we're going to drive him away right now!"

Committed to that view, Arne Johnson reached for the Bible on the coffee table. But before he could pick it up the book slid away. Challenged, Arne made the sign of the cross, allowing David to grab the small, worn Bible.

"Where is he now?" Arne asked David.

"Don't you see him? He's by the window—in front of the curtains." Only Debbie was able to make out a vague shadow of the figure.

"We'll get rid of him, one way or another," Arne declared, picking up a loaded Polaroid camera. "If they want proof this thing is here, we'll show 'em its picture!"

"Stop it, Cheyenne! He's telling you to cut it out!" David cried.

"Oh yeah? Tell him I'm gonna cut *him* out!" Arne put down the camera and picked up the bottle of holy water.

"*I* command you to begone, Satan. *I* command you to leave this house. Begone! *I* command you to leave," Arne stated, casting holy water at the curtains. Without realizing it, Arne was violating the essential precept that man can command such spirits only in the name of God. It was one of many sincere but tragic mistakes Arne would make in the case.

"Where is he now?" Arne asked.

"He's outside, looking in. He just tapped on the window."

"Good! Now we'll finish him off!" Arne declared with conviction. "I'm not going to read him any more psalms. I'm not going to read him any more bedtime prayers. I'm going to read him the Bible. I'll read it to him page by page, front to back. I'll read it to him until he can't stand it anymore!"

" 'In the beginning God created the heaven and the earth. And the earth was without form, and void; and darkness was upon the face of the deep. And the Spirit of God moved upon the face of the waters.' "

"It's not doing any good, Chey. He's back. See, he's in the rocking chair," David announced.

Apparently it was; they all saw the rocking chair suddenly moving back and forth.

"He's not there," Arne remarked defiantly.

A stomping sound was heard. "He just stamped on the floor with his hoofs," reported David. This was followed by three knocks.

"Okay," said Arne, "he gets another bath!" Arne

144

threw holy water on the chair, causing the rocking to stop.

Frustrated, Arne looked around the room, then suddenly he stood immobilized, gazing at the front door. For the first time, he saw the beast.

The manifestation was only that of the head, which appeared as big as the door. Its eyes were large and black and wholly consuming. It had high cheekbones, the semblance of a goatee, and sharp, broken teeth— evident because the figure was noiselessly laughing at him. The whole head glowed, changing from pink to brown to scarlet red. Upon being seen, the appalling countenance blurred into a globe of light, then dissipated.

"Look out, Cheyenne!" Debbie suddenly yelled out, as Arne spun around. The rocking chair was rising into the air.

"He's gonna throw it at you!" said David frantically.

Arne lurched forward and pressed the "levitating" chair back down to the floor.

"Behind you, Chey!" David warned. "He's coming at you. He's gonna punch you!"

Arne, now facing the center of the living room, reasoned that if the beast could punch him, then he could punch it back.

Seeing that Arne's hand was doubled up into a fist, David said, "He's five steps away . . . three steps . . . he's in front of you! Hit him *now!*"

Arne cocked his arm and let go with a forceful, blind swing. Suddenly his body went numb and was momentarily consumed by a fierce coldness.

"You got him! You hit him in the jaw! He fell down!" David announced, amazed.

Three knocks sounded from the far side of the room.

"Cheyenne, look! He's got David!" Judy cried.

Arne turned around to see David being pulled away, his tee-shirt yanked up from behind, his arms shooting straight into the air.

"Help me!" David pleaded, starting to rise off the floor. "He's gonna throw me!"

Arne cast two handfuls of the holy water in his direction. David was set back down squarely on his feet.

Suddenly the room turned cold. In a few minutes, however, the temperature returned to normal. But then the temperature kept climbing until it was uncomfortably hot. Within ten minutes, the temperature rose and fell seventy-five degress, before the atmosphere returned again to normal.

Activity also came to a stop, though not for the night. Calm reigned for about ninety minutes; then, as Debbie's journal indicates, David was attacked again:

> 5:00 A.M.: David just put his head to the pillow and he was out from exhaustion when this figure attacked him at 5:07 A.M., choking him. His eyes bugged out, and his tongue was hanging out, gasping for air. David tried to free his throat. We threw holy water on him and blessed him. We all witnessed this. We all wondered what [would happen] if we let him go through with the choking, but decided against it. What if we couldn't bring him out of it?

> 5:35 A.M.: David had the same identical attack as at 5:07 A.M.

5:40 A.M.: We all heard the humming sound like a space ship. David, Chey, and I went to the window. Outside there was a red spot floating in front of the fence. It suddenly vanished.

6:00 A.M.: David had the last attack, being punched in the left eye. We all heard the hit. It was hard. David finally went to sleep at 6:30 A.M.

The last entry was probably the most important, because Carl Glatzel was forced to see it.

Although Carl Glatzel had occasionally observed unexplainable incidents in his home, he refused to admit it, which angered his wife and children. Why didn't he help them? they wondered. Didn't he care?

In his heart, the matter grieved Carl deeply. But he didn't broadcast his emotions. The family looked to him for strength and guidance, and in his mind, acknowledgment of the problem was tantamount to encouraging their "foolishness." "Weak-minded people let this happen in their lives," he told them.

Besides, even though this chaos was undeniably taking place, Carl knew there wasn't a thing he could do about it. Arne was behaving exactly the way he would have behaved; and Judy was thinking the way he would have thought. There was nothing he could add.

But then Carl saw his son David get punched in the face with malicious, premeditated cruelty by an unseen coward that had the strength of a man and the wickedness of a maniac.

That was it. Visible or invisible, what had happened was wrong and had to be stopped.

"Judy, I want a priest in this house when I come home from work tonight," Carl said for the first time in his life, "and I don't want him to leave until this nightmare is over."

Chapter XV

That morning, as usual, Arne went out five minutes early to warm up Debbie's car before they left for work.

Debbie was preparing to leave when she heard David call to her from the living room. His voice was full of alarm as he asked her where Arne was.

When Debbie told him Arne was out in the car, David exclaimed, "No! He can't be out there! The beast . . . and the two helpers . . . they said they're gonna get back at him. They're gonna crack up the car!"

Outside, at the top of the steep driveway, Arne sat waiting for Debbie. Suddenly, unexpectedly, the engine started to race, although the car was in park and had been idling properly. Arne attempted to tap the gas pedal but found it was already pressed to the floor. He pulled the emergency brake and switched off the key. But it had no effect: the engine kept roaring.

Again he tried to tap the gas pedal and switch off the ignition. But the engine still raced madly. Arne reached for the door handle to get out—but it wouldn't work!

When he looked up again, he saw something standing halfway down the driveway. It was the beast. And it was pointing at a huge oak tree to the left of the driveway.

Suddenly the car jerked into motion. Within seconds it was careening down the driveway. Arne stood on the brakes, but they wouldn't work. Nor could he steer the car, which was hurtling straight toward the oak tree.

"The car was already heading down the hill when I got outside," Debbie said later. "The brake lights were on but the car wasn't stopping. Instead, the wheels on the left side went off the driveway and began tearing up the brush. It was heading for the trees at top speed. That's when the car went over."

Just moments before Arne would have collided with the big oak tree, the wheels on the left side bit into peat and soggy mulch, and the car tilted onto its side. It slid safely to a halt just feet from the tree, narrowly escaping what probably would have been a fatal crash.

Having gone through a night of hell and a morning of terror, the fear in the Glatzel house was virtually palpable the afternoon of Friday, August 1. Judy made urgent calls to the Warrens and the priests, explaining the havoc taking place and pleading that someone stay with the family that night, as the beast was apparently set to *kill* someone because of David's refusal to surrender his soul.

Father Grosso agreed to come to the house that night, followed by the Warrens later on. Judy was immensely relieved. But no sooner did she hang up the

A RECORD OF POSSESSION

The driveway
leading to
the Glatzel home
(Photo: Ed Warren)

The Glatzels'
home and
their snowmobiles
(Photo: Ed Warren)

Ed and Lorraine Warren in the Glatzel home with
David, Arne, Debbie, Alan, and Judy
(Photo: Dr. Anthony Giangrasso)

Judy and Carl Glatzel
(Photo: Tony Spera, T.C.B. Assoc.)

Arne and Debbie
(Photo: Alan Glatzel)

David celebrating his
twelfth birthday
on August 13, 1980
(Photo: Alan Glatzel)

David coming under possession
(Photo: Alan Glatzel)

David possessed
(Photo: Alan Glatzel)

The family rocking
chair in which
the beast often sat
(Photo: Arne Johnson)

Showing the strain of the situation, Ed Warren, Alan,
Arne, and Carl Glatzel are
seated at the family's kitchen table.
(Photo: John Kenyhercz)

Ed and Lorraine
Warren with David
during a peaceful
period following
a Mass in
the Glatzel home
(Photo: Debbie Glatzel)

David fighting off the
unseen hands
which are threatening
to strangle him
(Photo: Debbie Glatzel)

Struggling to control
David while
he is possessed
(Photo: Alan Glatzel)

St. Joseph's Convent in Brookfield,
the site of the second exorcism attempt
(Photo: Ed Warren)

Arne and Debbie trying to record David's words while
he is under possession
(Photo: Alan Glatzel)

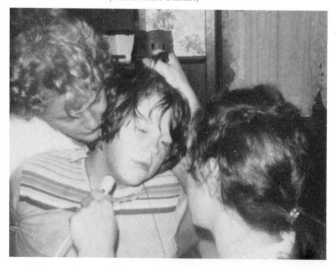

Brookfield Kennels where the murder occurred. Debbie and Arne lived in the apartment on the top floor.
(Photo: Alan Glatzel)

David undergoing possession

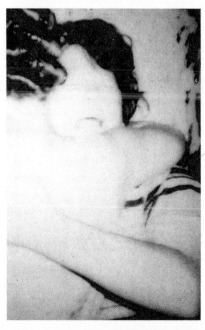

David hugging his mother after coming out from under possession
(Photo: Debbie Glatzel)

Arne coming out of the courthouse during his trial
(Photo: Gerald Brittle)

phone than she was faced with the fury of Carl, Jr., who had been eavesdropping on an extension phone.

"What the hell do you think you're doing? *I* don't want those stinking Warrens coming here!" he exclaimed. "And most of all, I don't want another Goddamn priest setting foot in my house!"

Judy was angry. "Mind your own business," she said to her fourteen-year-old son. "Anybody I say can come here. You talk like you've got an opinion, and you don't!"

"This is my house too. I got my rights. If one of them lousy bastards comes in here, I'll show him what a shotgun is good for," threatened the enraged boy, slamming every door in the house as he left. Immediately Judy checked the gun cabinet, in which were stored half-a-dozen shotguns and hunting rifles. It was locked and no guns were missing.

What did concern Judy, however, was that the beast and its helpers might suddenly play possum because help was on the way. But that proved not to be the case. Trouble started again at 6:05 P.M., with three resounding knocks on the front door. Innocently, David answered the door, with Debbie right behind him. No one was there.

Half an hour later, Carl Glatzel came home from work, drawn and haggard like the rest of the family. He was relieved to learn that one of the priests from St. Joseph's was coming that night.

Father Grosso had spent the day reading demonology. He found it to be an interesting area of theology, but he remained unconvinced of its validity.

The heat wave that characterized the summer of 1980 was at its peak in August. When Father Grosso turned into the Glatzels' driveway shortly after 9:00 P.M., a steamy fog was rising off the pond in the front of the property. He parked his car beside the others at the top of the driveway, then got out and stood for a moment looking at the house. The scene was so normal, so contemporary, and essentially unthreatening.

Father Grosso took one step toward the front door. Suddenly the air was filled with a vicious, rolling animal growl. The priest felt himself in jeopardy. He stood frozen in place, listening for the approach of an unfriendly animal, but now all he heard were the familiar sounds of frogs and crickets. Father Grosso took a few cautious steps, then proceeded to the front door without further incident.

Alan answered the door. After introductions were made Father Grosso was shown a seat in the living room. Carl and Judy Glatzel, their sons, and Arne, Debbie, and Jason were waiting. Strangely, Carl, Jr., behaved courteously, at least for a few minutes; then, before Father Grosso could begin speaking, something took the boy over.

"Look, I'm gonna tell you this once—these people are all crazy," he said getting up out of his chair. "They're making all this up—every bit of it. Nothing's wrong in this house but *them*! For the last month they've been driving me nuts with their ghosts and fairy tales. Get them a doctor, or call the cops: that's what they need. But I'm not gonna sit here and listen to them lie anymore. They make me sick. Really sick!" The boy then left the living room in a huff.

David's behavior, too, suddenly changed when the priest asked, "How are you tonight, David?"

David shook his head, and with a sneer looked at Judy and said, "Get that blimp out of here!"

"Is that the way you ordinarily speak to a priest?" Father Grosso asked.

"You? You call yourself a priest? Hah! Don't make me laugh!" David stated to the humiliation of all.

With this welcome, Father Grosso had considerable difficulty feeling any compassion for these people. Yet, he stuck it out, and for the next forty-five minutes asked the family some tough questions, tinged with skepticism, that made him sound more like a psychologist than a priest. Had David been sick or experienced mental problems? Was David under medication? Had David and Carl been happy children? Did the Glatzels severely punish the boys? Was there alcoholism or drug abuse in the house? Did the boys like horror movies? Did they fight with other children in the neighborhood? Finally, the priest insinuated that the family was overreacting to a series of isolated, ordinary events.

The Glatzels felt insulted. It seemed obvious the priest didn't believe anything about the case.

Arne, being the "outsider," stood up for the family and told Father Grosso of their attempts to resolve matters through faith and religious means. Debbie backed up Arne's statements by reading extracts from her journal that week.

"What do you think, Carl?" Father Grosso asked. "Do you have an explanation for this?"

"I don't know what's causing it," said Carl, "but I can tell you it's happening. All you've got to do is take one look at that kid's body—he's all marked up from being beaten by *something*. I don't know what that something is, but the marks are there."

Father Grosso got up and walked over to where David sat in the rocking chair. The priest was about three steps from the boy when suddenly a coarse snarling issued from the boy's body.

Father Grosso turned white. He slowly backed away and sat down in his chair again.

"Who did that?" asked the priest, visibly shaken.

"Don't you know?" David replied. "You heard it outside, didn't you?"

The priest was speechless.

"What happened outside?" Carl Glatzel demanded.

"The beast was outside when he came in," David revealed. "He growled at him when he started to walk toward the house."

Carl looked to Father Grosso for a reply. "That's true," said the priest, nodding in confirmation. His firm skepticism had suddenly been shattered.

Trying to get a better understanding, the priest then questioned David about the number, origin, appearance, and motives of the alleged entities.

At first David refused to answer, fearing an attack by the beast. But Judy convinced her son that Father Grosso was there to help. David lived in abject terror and wanted an end to the problem more than anyone. Therefore, he opened up and told the priest that none of the entities were human; that he'd never seen anything like the beast in real life; that he hated all of them, especially the beast; and that most of all he wanted them to go away.

David even gave out some information that the family had never heard. The entities drew strength from heat, and preferred to stay on the hot roof or in the attic. Amazingly, he revealed why Judy always found the kitchen chairs pulled away from the table: the entities sat there and had "meetings," in which they discussed what to do next, in languages David could not understand. When in the house, they always surrounded the family in a circle and chanted, which resulted in the arguments that had been so common the last month. He told how the beast dispatched the helpers to work and to check things out for him. An entity was posted as a sentinel at the base of the driveway; on the corner of Silvermine Road; at Pocono Road; by the railroad bridge; by the Congregational Church; others traveled back and forth between Brookfield and the rental property in Newtown.

Whenever a family member left the house, he was always accompanied by one or more helpers. The beast often accompanied David's father to work; the entities liked Carl and left him alone because he was a "sucker"— having not been baptized. Because they were now involved, entities were with all the priests and the Warrens as well.

The beast spat in the family's food; stroked the women's thighs; shut off the hot water and air-conditioning; caused the family pets to fight; banged on the walls; threw the holy candles. It used young Carl to express its will, and claimed to "own" David's soul. The entities hated Jesus; they hated Christmas; they hated people; they hated each other; and they always spoke of death. Further, from what David could make out, someone was going to be stabbed with a knife, and the name most frequently mentioned was Arne's.

Except for the beast, their appearance did not change. They did not have to eat or drink or go to the bathroom. They knew about the past; they knew about the future; they knew the contents of books; they even watched the television. They definitely had a mind, asserted David, and the only way to change it was through "exorcism."

David, speaking in terms and concepts that even he didn't understand, had suddenly said too much. Right there, in front of the priest, the boy was choked.

"Help, mommy, he's trying to kill me!" were the last words David managed to utter.

Father Grosso was appalled. The child was being

strangled right there in front of him. Judy began shaking the boy, while the priest dug into his black travel bag and took out holy oil he'd brought "just in case." Applying the oil to David's forehead, Father Grosso prayed aloud over the child in Latin.

The choking stopped, but David went wild. He thrashed and screamed at the "pain" the priest caused him. When Father Grosso started to approach, David's eyes were those of a crazed animal, and the vicious, unnatural growling filled the room.

"Get away from me!" said a coarse, manlike voice inside David, who then broke free and ran into his bedroom. The scene was one of sudden pandemonium, and Father Grosso was terrified. So was Carl Glatzel, who had never witnessed these hideous sieges before.

With true courage, the priest took his black bag down the hallway to find David, in order to render a proper blessing on him. But when the child—or rather that which was affecting the child—laid eyes on the priest, growling filled the room and he was forced to back away.

Shaken, Father Grosso returned to the living room, sat down with the rest of the frightened family, and began asking pertinent questions. Talking to them now as people with a valid problem, he came to understand the scope of their awful fears.

At 11:30 P.M. the Warrens arrived and were introduced to Carl Glatzel, whom they'd never met before. The Warrens were not surprised to learn that David had come under attack in front of the priest; however, what did concern them was the intensity of the outbreak and the fierceness of David's response.

Ed Warren and Father Grosso went back to the bedroom to speak with David. The doubting, prove-it-to-me look on the young priest's face was now gone.

They found David lying face down on his bed. A variety of hissing and groaning noises were emanating from his body. Ed entered first; Father Grosso followed cautiously and stood by the foot of the bed. Although David hadn't so much as looked up, the snarling of an animal sounded as soon as the priest entered the room behind Ed.

"I thought I told you to stay the fuck away from here, Warren," said an adulterated voice in the child. Suddenly David's arm swung up and caught Ed Warren with a back-hand in the face.

Stepping out of range, Ed asked, "Who's speaking, anyway?" There was no answer.

"All right, then I'm talking to you, David," Ed said. "Father Grosso is going to help you. He's going to . . ."

Both men were aghast as David, without so much as moving a muscle, levitated off the bed some three feet—his back to the ceiling—then landed feet-first on the floor. He turned and ran out the door and locked himself in the bathroom.

Lest David harm himself with razors or other implements, Ed Warren got Carl Glatzel to unlock the bathroom door.

"Please excuse me, Father," David said in a demure voice as he walked back into his bedroom. Reality, to the priest, had been turned inside out. How could these people cope with it? he wondered.

Father Grosso was genuinely shocked at what he saw. Virtually every incident he'd experienced with David was bizarre and patently unnatural. "You were right," the priest told Ed Warren as they hastened out of the room. "These things do happen. I believe it now."

The Warrens stayed another hour that night, speaking with the family and Father Grosso about recent statements the entity had made, and reviewing the incidents of the past few days.

Afterwards, Carl Glatzel and Father Grosso walked out to the car with the Warrens. Their impression of Carl was that he was a stable, physically strong man, of good moral character, and that he enjoyed the respect of his family.

"You hear about these things in books and in the movies," he said to Father Grosso and the Warrens, "but you never think they could happen to you."

"What do you think is causing the problem? Do you think it's the result of an excitable family?" asked Lorraine.

"No, I don't believe that."

"Have you ever seen David behave like that in the past?" she asked.

"What I saw in there is not my son," Carl replied. "David is a gentle kid. He never raises his voice, and he gets along with everyone. Now he's acting like some kind of monster. He talks about stuff I don't even understand, and I'm his father. There's something wrong, something *really* wrong!"

"What about these entities David speaks about?" Father Grosso asked. "Do you believe him?"

Carl looked up to the house, then took a few paces out of earshot. "Yes, I believe him. In fact, I know he's telling the truth."

"How do you know?" Father Grosso asked.

The time had come for Carl Glatzel, and he had to weigh his personal pride against his son's need for help. "I know because I've *seen* this entity he calls the beast. And he's seen me. I saw it the night you—Mr. and Mrs. Warren—came here the first time, back in the middle of July.

"When I sleep, I sleep. Nothing wakes me up. The

158

night you were here, I was sound asleep. I'd been putting in overtime just to stay away from this madhouse, so I was exhausted.

"Well, for no reason at all, that night I woke up. Wide awake. I knew I was awake because I looked at my watch. It was exactly quarter after one in the morning. A second later I thought, that's strange, how could I look at my watch without turning on the lights? Yet the whole room was completely lit up with a bright, bluish light. The wall switch was off and so were the lamps.

"I sat up, trying to figure out the source of the light. That's when I saw it—a face on the wall. Not a human face. This was something else. It was a head, maybe two feet across, about the size of one of these round patio tables. The thing was hairy, and the face was glowing red. It had a beard. Its ears were set close to the head. It had a nose, a mustache, and big, coal-black eyes that blinked. I can't say it scared me; I can say I had doubts about what I was seeing. So I glanced away, just to test myself, but when I looked back, the face was still there.

"Then I got annoyed, mostly with myself. What is this, I thought, am I in a dream? I checked my watch again. It was around one-seventeen. I listened, and I could hear talking out in the kitchen. Then I knew I really was awake. I looked again, and that face was still on the wall. But this time I saw it had jagged teeth; I could tell because it was giving me this hell-raising smile—like it was saying, 'I'm doing this to you, turkey, and there ain't a damn thing you can do to stop it.'

"After that it faded away; so did the light in the room. I lay back down, but the next thing I knew, I felt a couple of solid whallops hit the floor of the house from underneath. Too strange for me, I said: I'm not even

159

going to think about this! That was it: I fell back asleep, and the next time I woke up it was dawn.

"What got to me during the week was that the kids talked about seeing the same thing, and they described it the same way—black eyes, broken teeth, a beard, the works. Since that time I've caught sight of something strange skulking around in the woods out back, but I never saw it long enough to make sense out of it, so I didn't pay it any heed."

"Was there anything said tonight, by anyone, that wasn't true, or was exaggerated for effect?" Lorraine asked.

"No," Carl answered, "they're telling it the way it is, unfortunately. Why should they lie, anyway? They're up with this night after night, saying prayers, fighting with David, and so on. It's like a war in there. That's the only way I can describe it."

"There really is a method to the madness taking place here. It is a spirit, but it's not a ghost. What's entrenched itself is a very powerful intelligence of an *in*human order. What everyone is experiencing is *diabolical* phenomena. In other words, Mr. Glatzel, what we're dealing with here is the devil," Lorraine said.

After a long pause, Carl asked, "What's the next step?"

"That will be up to Father Grosso and the Church authorities," Lorraine replied. "Technically, our job is done, though we'll stay with you till the end. Our work is to determine if there is in fact validity to a case. In this circumstance, I'm sorry to say, there *is* validity."

"Bringing an end to the disturbance, however, is a different story," Ed said. "There are methods to deal with the problem, but in the long run there's no guarantee of success. Ultimately, it depends on the strength and power of the entity involved, and on the effectiveness of the religious procedures used to expel it. Make no mistake, though, what's in your house is enormously dangerous—to you, to your family, and to the clergy who must confront it—and there's no room for error. A mistake or miscalculation in judgment can result in serious injury, ruined lives, or even death."

Chapter XVI

The Brookfield case was out of control. The beast and its pernicious legion had invaded the lives of the Glatzel family, and no form of resistance could make them leave.

The case worsened not by discernible jumps but through a constant intensification of pressure. By the first week of August 1980, life in the Glatzel home was a combination of fear, fatigue, and phenomena that pushed every member of the family to the brink of human endurance.

There was no relief, no let-up. That which couldn't have been happening took place every day boldly and with impunity. Emotions in the family were raw. Crankiness seemed to be turbocharged into ferocious anger and hatred by the invading entities. And perhaps the worst affected was young Carl, who maintained a hostile and contrary opinion on everything. The prime targets of his hatred were Judy and Debbie. He contradicted everything they said. When one of them would seek to defend herself verbally, Carl would attack her physically. There were bruises all over their bodies from repeated punches.

At the core of his behavior was an attempt to suppress the truth about the chaos in his home.

"Say it isn't so! Say you're lying! Say that nothing is happening!" he commanded, threatening them with violence.

As Ed Warren notes, "Truth is the enemy. Denial of the truth is the way of the devil, and young Carl's behavior was a classic illustration of that fact."

But David was a much worse problem. The oppression inflicted on him was succeeding.

Hour after hour, day in and day out, for over a month, David was the target for a cruel, determined attack by the irrational forces of darkness that had taken over the home. By the middle of the first week of August, David had reached the end of his endurance. A distinct change was coming over him.

He had resisted and resisted and resisted, and resisted again, and now he had nothing left. Devoid of emotion, weakened, frightened, threatened, and robbed of all semblance of his normal self, David Glatzel had become spiritually destitute. The little boy which the family knew as their giggly, charming teddy-bear, who had a passion for dirt piles and told them elephant jokes he learned in the *Weekly Reader*, was no longer there. David's spirit was gone. His body rendered little more than a breathing shell, he was ready to be taken. Ready to be made "like them"; ready to be made into an automaton of evil.

Thus, on August 6, 1980, David Michael Glatzel was possessed by the devil.

The final descent into tragedy began when the

three priests from St. Joseph's Church in Brookfield began to take an active interest in stopping the assaults on the child. Not only had they recommended exorcism, but almost every day after August 1, one of the three young priests came to the Glatzel home to render assistance through prayers and blessings. But when the priests went away, the attacks on the child became even more brutal.

Sleep was a luxury David did not enjoy. Torment was the child's only plight. Indeed, the night before the first full possession occurred, David screamed wildly in pain at the kitchen table as the entities, in a terrifying display of unnatural power, forcibly turned his head around 180 degrees until the boy was looking *backwards!*

What more could they do to the child, Judy asked in tearful desperation? The following morning she found out.

At dawn on the morning of August 6, David was limp and weary. For the first time in a long while, he went into his bedroom and fell soundly asleep. After Arne and Debbie had dragged themselves up and out to work, Judy took a nap. To her relief, David was still sleeping when she got up. In fact, he was even snoring so hard he sounded like a pig.

An hour later, David screamed out in his sleep, "Help! Mommy! Save me!" There was total desperation to his plea, and Judy tried to wake him. But he did not rouse. She backed off in fright when a dog-like snarl issued from his body. Judy was distraught but there was nothing she could do.

Around noon, she heard sounds of groaning and awful tortured moans coming from David's bedroom. "David?" she called out fearfully, but she got no answer. "David?" she called again, walking halfway to the bedroom. Then she stopped. The repugnant smell of vomit met her, and she could hear vague whisperings in the air.

"David? David, answer me!" she demanded.

Deep, raucous laughter suddenly issued from the bedroom.

Judy gasped and backed away. She began to feel a dread sense of doom—the kind that comes when one knows something awful has happened. Yet, this was Judy's son, and she had to act. She drew a deep breath and took the final, fateful steps to the door at the end of the hall.

Courageously, she pushed open the bedroom door, stepped across the threshold, and looked at her son.

Her knees buckled. What Judy Glatzel saw she will never, never forget.

What sat there only barely resembled David. His whole face had *physically* changed. His head was bloated. His cheekbones were set higher. His nose, once slender, was pushed in and wide, with the nostrils pointing upward like a pig's. His lips were swollen, and foamy saliva surrounded his mouth and ran down his chin. His half-open mouth was frozen in a grimace of hate; his tongue hung out. The muscles around his eyes were contracted, causing them to look squinted and narrow. His irises no longer had color; they were all black. His head wove back and forth. He sat in the middle of the bed, with his arms hanging down as though they were broken or paralyzed.

Judy Glatzel said nothing. She just stood staring in disbelief at the terrible, abominable scene. She was beyond tears, beyond fear.

"Who are you?" she finally asked with utter contempt.

Coarse laughter was the only reply.

"David?" she asked desperately. "Is . . . is that *you*, David?"

The creature sat staring at Judy through glassy, unblinking eyes. The scene turned her stomach.

From the direction of David's body came a hoarse voice. *"David's not here!"* The lips did not move.

"What?" she cried in panic.

"David's gone . . . His soul . . . is mine!" the slow, deep voice proclaimed.

Judy screamed hysterically, backing out of the room. Then she dropped to her knees in the hall and began to cry the deep tears of ruination.

Alan came running through the back door, having heard his mother screaming. He found her sobbing on the floor of the hall.

Judy looked up with a tear-stained face. "David . . . go look at him! Look at my baby . . . my beautiful baby. . . ."

Alan thought David was dead. He strode into the bedroom, and seconds later emerged as white as a sheet.

"Is it me, Alan?" Judy asked, with hope in her voice. "Say it's me, Alan. Tell me that's not happening! Tell me! Tell me it's not so!"

Choking back his own tears, Alan answered, "I can't mom. It's real. I saw it too."

Another bestial groan came from the bedroom, filling Judy and Alan with total fright.

Alan got his mother to her feet and led her back to the kitchen. Trembling with fear, neither knew what to do. Finally, after a long silence, Alan went to the phone, wanting to call his father and a priest. But then he saw the Warrenses' number posted by the phone. He dialed nervously.

"Mr. Warren, this is Alan Glatzel. Uh . . . you

better talk to my mother," he said, suddenly drawing a blank.

Swallowing hard, Judy cleared her throat before taking the phone. "Do you remember one night you said that David wasn't possessed because if he was, we'd know it? Well, he is now! That thing possessed him. In fact, it told me David isn't even here! He looks hideous. He . . . Oh, my God! He's coming out of the room toward us! . . . Come quick!"

In seconds the possessed child was in front of his mother. He grabbed the phone from her hand and threw it on the floor.

"You foul slut!" It was the man's voice, speaking through David's mouth. *"You know what you deserve, don't you? Don't you, bitch? You deserve to die!"*

Immediately his hands clamped around Judy's neck. Alan stood aghast until he realized that the possessing entity in David was trying to kill his mother. He broke the stranglehold, only to have the vindictive fury turned on him.

The entity stalked Alan around the room with violent determination. When it got Alan cornered, it began swinging its fists and spitting profusely in the boy's face. Grunts and screeching noises could be heard coming out of David's body as well. Judy grabbed David's flailing arms from behind and stopped the attack. But the thing in David was wild and snarling like a dog, and whipped around, trying to bite Judy's wrist to break her hold.

Alan, maneuvered the kitchen chairs until he and Judy were on one side of the kitchen table and it was on the other.

Panting like an animal with its tongue hanging out, the entity stared at them with vicious rage. *"I hate you,"* it said.

"*We hate you,*" said another.

"There's two of them!" Alan cried.

"*Hah! If you only knew, fat boy,*" it replied ominously.

"Who are you? *What* are you?" Alan asked the perverted image of his brother.

But the entity in David paid no attention to Alan. It was concerned only with getting its hands on him and Judy.

"Where's my brother?" Alan demanded.

"*We have him,*" it answered.

"Where? Where is he?" Alan insisted.

"*In hell!*" it yelled.

The kitchen was a battle scene, with chairs knocked over and the table shoved awkwardly into the center of the room. Yet, the table was positioned in such a way that Judy could reach over and grab the bottle of holy water that she kept on the counter.

"I don't think you like this, do you?" Judy asked breathlessly, hoping she was doing the right thing.

"*You wouldn't dare!*" it said, backing up.

"Oh yes I would," Judy said. "Where is my son? Give my son David back!"

"Never!"

Judy poured holy water into her hand, then threw it at the possessed body of her son.

The action caused wild screams and whoops of pain. Everywhere the water landed, welts and splotches of redness appeared.

"*It burns . . . it burns,*" a woman's voice shrieked out of the child.

Immediately the thing retreated back down the hall and into David's bedroom.

Neither Alan nor Judy said a word: they were too overwhelmed. The phone receiver lay on the floor, buzzing senselessly; Alan picked it up and replaced it on the hook.

A voice then called out, "Mommy! Mommy, I don't feel good." It was David!

Impulsively, Judy started down the hallway to help her son, ignoring Alan's warning: "That's not David! That's not his voice!"

As soon as she got to the doorway, the deranged thing stepped out, grabbed her by her breasts, yanked her into the room, and began trying to strangle her again.

"You fucking blond whore," roared the man's voice. *"I'll show you. I'll rip your face off. I'll break your goddamn neck. I'll kill you and kill you!"*

Alan raced to his mother's aid, but the moment he got near the possessing thing, he was knocked back with a well-aimed punch in the jaw. At the same instant, though, Judy pulled herself free and fled down the hallway to the kitchen, with Alan right behind. They were not pursued. Laughter echoed out of the room, punctuating the horror.

Unable to endure another physical bout, Judy and Alan ran out the back door and into the bright light of day.

"Why? Why? Why?" Judy cried. But Alan had no answer. He merely tried to console her by putting his arm around her shoulder as she wept.

Soon a black car came roaring up the Glatzel's driveway. Ed and Lorraine Warren jumped out and rushed to Judy and Alan.

"Where is he?" Ed asked, immediately.

"In the house," Judy replied. "You better not go in there alone. He's dangerous."

Judy needn't have made that last statement. The Warrens had seen possession before, and it was always the same: foul, ugly, and extremely dangerous. Without saying any more, the Warrens entered the house.

"Where is he, Lorraine?" Ed asked his wife, relying on her clairvoyance.

"He's in the living room," Lorraine replied instantly. "This is a bad one Ed," she added.

The Warrens walked through the kitchen and over to the living-room doorway. There, sitting in the rocking chair that the beast had claimed as its own, with his head bowed down and his chin on his chest, was the possessed child. Yet, the horrid spectacle of his takeover was not readily apparent until Ed Warren called David by name. Then, the entity in the child slowly looked up at the Warrens, and the tragedy became clear. David's face was totally transformed. What looked out at them was a being of a different order.

"Oh my Lord," Lorraine muttered, backing off and turning away.

The worst had happened, and there was nothing the Warrens could do, other than to observe and confirm that possession had occurred.

"David, can you speak to me?" Ed asked.

The thing stared at Ed, projecting intense hatred.

"I want to speak to David," Ed insisted.

"Get out of my house!" the possessing entity said finally.

"I want to speak to David," Ed pressed.

"No!".

"Who are you?"

"I am the one who visited you. I am the one who scattered the pictures."

The reference was meaningful because Ed had found the photos and paperwork on the Glatzel case scattered around his office earlier in the week. The thing had evidently visited him in spirit form.

"Are you alone?" Ed asked.

After a silence came the enigmatic answer, *"We are many."*

"How many? How many of you are there in that child?"

"Forty and three."

"Who's in charge?"

"I am!" It obviously took umbrage at the question.

"How do I know that you're not David?" Ed challenged.

There was a tennis ball in the middle of the floor. The entity in David looked down at the ball and pointed. The tennis ball immediately whizzed across the room and bounced off a far wall.

"You have stolen this child's body," Lorraine accused. "His body does not belong to you. David has a right to . . ."

"Shut your filthy yap, you strutting harlot!"

"You aren't going to get away with possessing this boy. We won't allow it," Ed said.

"Who will stop me?" it said defiantly.

"The priests will drive you away."

"No priest will drive me away!"

"That's true," Ed said. "But the power of God is stronger than you *or* me. And through the power of God, through the power of Christ, you will be sent back to where you came from!"

Ed Warren's statement had only one effect: it enraged the entity. It suddenly spewed a profusion of unthinkable blasphemies directed against God, Jesus, and Mary. And with each vulgar proclamation, the thing worked itself up into a higher and more irrational state of vehemence.

Then suddenly the verbal sewage stopped. A gross gagging replaced the torrent of invectives. The eyes then rolled back into the head; David's body shuddered all over; and, as the Warrens watched, the features of the boy's face physically transformed back to normal.

"What are you doing here?" David asked the Warrens a minute later.

"Don't you know, David?"

"No, I just woke up."

Chapter XVII

What began on July 2, 1980, with the warning: *Beware!* progressed rapidly through the classic stages of encroachment, infestation, internal oppression, and external oppression, in a steadily worsening stream of activity that culminated in the diabolical possession of David Glatzel.

Although what happened to David was rare, it was not unique. Every century has noteworthy cases of possession; indeed, a major case of diabolical possession takes place somewhere in the world every decade. The phenomenon of possession is always characterized by intense religious blasphemy, violent hatred of human beings, and horrific displays of unnatural power.

Hell had literally descended on the Glatzel family. Daily, from August 6 on, David was possessed with impunity by one or more vulgar, blaspheming spirits. And, whether physical or mental, the outrage went about as far as it could go. One possessing entity in the child repeatedly told Judy how "sexy" she was, and made other lascivious remarks both to her and to Debbie, causing the women to fear they might suddenly be victims of some kind of terrible, perverse attack.

The beast, when possessing David, railed on with stilted justifications for possessing the boy, asserting it had every right to his soul and his body. It made hideous remarks about Christ and Mary and loosed torrents of profanities against them. It claimed nothing could drive it away; no matter how hard they might try, the priests would fail to dislodge it. In the end, *it* would drive away the priests.

The Glatzels hated this monstrous thing, and it hated them. Yet, cloaked in David's body, they could not strike it; as a spirit they could not kill it; and with the strength it exhibited, they only got hurt when they fought it. It was the boss, like a terrorist holding a hostage. The best the family could do was keep from enraging the thing, lest it injure them or kill David.

"Once possession set in," said Lorraine Warren, "the Glatzel home was the scene of constant pandemonium. With eight people living in the house, each one was affected by the event in his own way. Sorrow, depression, and tears became the way of life. But it wasn't just David causing all the trouble. Once things got going, this negative force began to overwhelm young Carl, too. When the entity possessed David, it would invariably attack someone physically. And there young Carl would be, right in the middle of the fray—laughing hysterically, and cheering it on. He'd even join in the beatings. It was horrible, inconceivable. Both women were battered. David was battered and marked. Alan and Jason were battered. And Arne was not only battered; the thing in David was actually out to get him!

"Thank God Arne was there. He was the peacemaker. Other than Mr. Glatzel—who was working most of the time—Arne was the only person physically big enough to put up useful resistance. And Arne was never afraid of this thing—he saw it for what it was. If he hadn't been present in the house, the Glatzels will tell you, someone would definitely have been killed. The beast was a spirit of death, and Arne Johnson was constantly frustrating its attempts to take the life of a family member. Is it any wonder the thing launched a vendetta against him?"

The most disappointing development for the Glatzel family at this time was the lack of official help they received from Church authorities.

"By the beginning of August, the case had become the responsibility of the Diocese of Bridgeport, with specific responsibility residing with the bishop and his advisors. But what did they do for the Glatzels? Absolutely nothing!" declared Ed Warren. The family was left out in the proverbial wilderness.

"Chancery officials actually knew about the Brookfield case within a week after it started, in July. At that time, seeing trouble could develop, I wanted to have David put in a Catholic hospital where steps could be taken to 'treat' the problem," Ed Warren said. "But that suggestion was blocked. Then I wanted to bring in an exorcist from the Midwest to help the family. But because he'd be coming from outside the diocese, that got vetoed too. In the end, no action was taken until *after* the lid blew off and the child was possessed.

"The whole load, therefore, was placed on the three newly ordained priests in Brookfield. These young priests saw what was happening in the home, and they were extremely upset by it. What Father Grosso witnessed in the Glatzel home changed his whole outlook on life. The other two priests were similarly affected;

and I should also say disenchanted by how their superiors were handling the matter. You could see the disappointment in their eyes. It was an overwhelming ordeal for each of them. Almost every day Judy called the rectory, begging and pleading for help. The priests would immediately rush down to the house, day or night, and confront the entity. But their hands were tied. The case required major exorcism—they knew that. However, they were not exorcists; and even if they had been, the Rituale Romanum was called for in such a case, and that can only be performed with the express permission of the bishop of the diocese. This bishop wouldn't even answer my phone calls.

"Finally, matters grew so bad, and the pressure became so intense, that on August eighth or ninth, Fathers Grosso and Millea went directly to Bishop Curtis and requested that exorcism procedures be considered for David Glatzel as soon as possible. Fortunately, word came down a few days later to start assembling paperwork and to advise the family of the steps they'd have to take in order for major exorcism to be conducted. The directive was totally insensitive, of course: the family was fighting for their life against a devil, and the Church was playing politics. Nevertheless, it was at least a step forward. On August 11, I gave Father Grosso tape-recordings and photographs of the child under both oppression and possession, plus a support letter testifying to the fact that preternatural phenomena were occurring in the Glatzel home. Dr. Giangrasso also submitted a report detailing his evaluation of David's physical condition. Father Grosso then passed all this material on to chancery officials for their review."

This seemed to be a significant step, but the Glatzels were still living in torment, and the seeds of a profound tragedy were being sown. They were left to their own devices to cope with a grave problem about which they knew almost nothing. Consequently, mistakes were made, although they were made with the best intentions. In time, the bill would come due.

Arne Johnson continually resisted the malicious entity that possessed and persecuted David. He saw it as a bully and a coward and he told it so. At every turn he blocked its violent actions and defended David. Arne had no tolerance for the entity. He challenged it; in fact, he commanded it to leave. With all the verve of an exorcist, he commanded it to begone. And that was his mistake.

On the night of August 12, David was being whipped as punishment for wearing a new set of scapulars. He had already gone through three sets. For a while they had put rosary beads around David's neck for ptotection, but in the morning they were tied in knots around his throat.

That night David ripped the scapulars off his neck, declaring, *"My father doesn't want these fucking damn G-strings on me! Don't do it again! I obey my father! I don't obey you! You are foul! You are filth! We will make you die in hell for what you do!"*

David was under possession again.

"You son-of-a-bitching blond bastard bitching bitching foul female fool. . . . You skank . . . You rank skank . . . You . . . "

"Stop it, David!" Carl Glatzel ordered.

But David wasn't there. The rage escalated to a fury of crude defamations. Eyes ablaze, the possessing entity in David soon began talking so fast that it couldn't even be understood. Ranting and crazed with hatred, the thing started moving toward Judy to pounce and beat on her. Carl Glatzel stepped forward and blocked its move.

"Enough!" he yelled, slapping the frenzied face.

But it wasn't David, and suddenly the perverse fury was focused on Carl. Spitting out invectives, it raised its arms to strike Carl, but Carl grabbed it by the wrists. What should have been a weak-limbed child, however, immediately snapped free. A tussle ensued, and Carl Glatzel found himself fighting a creature whose strength equaled his own.

"Get out of my son! Get out!" Judy shrieked.

"*Never!*" it roared, gaining even more strength as it struggled. Carl spun David's body around and caught him in a powerful bear hug. Squeals and gasps came out of David's body as Carl squeezed with force equal to his anger.

"Carl! Stop it! You'll kill him! You'll break his ribs!" Judy cried frantically. Carl released his hold, but the boy's body had been rendered inert. Carl dragged David over to a chair and slapped him awake.

"Can I have a glass of ice water, mommy?" asked David, as though nothing had happened.

Judy, relieved that the bout was over, got David a glass of ice water.

"Thank you, mommy," said David, taking the glass, then throwing the water in her face. Raucous laughter came from the boy's body.

The night had begun.

Judy called the Warrens and told them the possessing entity was in David and it wasn't going away. They said they'd be right over, and told Judy to call the rectory immediately.

Upon phoning St. Joseph's rectory, Judy was told of the efforts being made to get an exorcism for David. One of the things her son required was a psychiatric evaluation. An appointment had already been made for the next day, with a doctor in lower Fairfield County.

When Judy returned to the living room, David was sitting bolt upright, staring at Carl. As Judy entered, the gaze was diverted to her. "I don't want them Warrens coming here! They turn my stomach! You got that, blondie?" The statement was totally disarming. Judy had made the call in the far end of the house with the door closed. "And we're going to the doctor, are we? Doctor Doolittle, Do-little. Do-shit. He won't believe you. You'll see! I'll make a fool out of you!"

"You'll make a fool out of yourself," Judy retorted.

"I'll watch!"

"That's right—you don't have the guts to show yourself to someone who counts. Get out of my son. Get out! Go back to hell where you come from!"

And so it went. It was a constant, ugly battle and there was no relief from it.

Usually, whenever the Warrens or the priests were called in, David was subjected to attack before they arrived—and after they left. It was no different this night. The form of torment this time was clubbing. David's body rolled around on the floor, jolted from the strikes. The situation was totally out of control.

Arne Johnson couldn't tolerate the injustice. His heart went out to the child. Accordingly, he took it upon himself to resist the entity and defend David from attack. Arne truly became the devil's adversary.

Standing over David, now lying on his back on the floor, Arne declared, "I command you to leave this child's body! Now!"

"*Get laid.*"

"I *command* you to leave this boy's body!"

"*You* . . . command . . . *shit!*" it replied with a sneer.

"I command you! Jesus commands you! God commands you! We all command you to leave!"

181

"You are shit! Jesus is shit! God is shit! You are all shit! You are all the same! You are shit! I command shit!" it responded with its own twisted logic, followed by coarse laughter.

"You're afraid of Jesus. You're nothing but a beast! An animal! I'll always work against you. The only power you have is to hurt little boys."

"Shut up! Shut up! Shut up!" it roared, enraged.

"What's the matter? Am I getting to you? Huh?" Arne said, keeping up the pressure. "Such a big shot! Picking on little kids, you low-life. Why don't you do it to me? Huh? Do it to me! Afraid you've met your match?"

"I'll kill you!"

"You won't kill anybody. I won't let you."

"You can't command me! I'm more than you could ever dream to be! I'll ruin you! I'll destroy you!"

In the middle of this intense confrontation, the Warrens arrived. The entity in David promptly went berserk.

"Get out of here! Get out! Get the shittin' hell out of here! You have no right to be here! I am in charge! Take that slut whore bitch with you! I've had enough of you! Get out! Get out!"

The Warrens were prepared for this, and Ed, without saying a word, hit it in the face with a spray of holy water. Immediately, it backed away from them, screaming and howling. As Ed Warren put it, "You don't fool around with a thing like that. It's no good, period. You don't let it talk. You don't let it think or act. A possessing entity has no business being in a person, and you use the powers you have at your command to make it as miserable as possible, until it's driven away."

After whimpering and groaning for a while, David

fell asleep. An hour later, as he was sleeping face down on the sofa, they noticed that his arms were "drifting" up into the air. Soon his legs drifted up too, leaving the boy in a bowed position on his stomach. His legs then began turning, one clockwise, the other counterclockwise. The activity continued for ten minutes.

Just after midnight trouble started again. First, David's left arm rose in the air. Then he began getting kicked in the head, which woke him. The kicks were repeated every few seconds.

"Stop it! Stop it now!" Arne commanded the invisible forces in the room. The blows to the head stopped. However, some other gross entity was manifesting through the boy now, speaking a gibberish language that sounded like English spoken backward—not an uncommon characteristic of possession.

"Who are you?" Debbie asked, looking into her brother's crazed eyes.

The answer did not come in the form of words. Instead, a red blotch appeared on David's right leg. The blotch quickly sharpened in detail until the reply was shockingly apparent: the face of a devil was emblazened on David's leg! After ten minutes, the blotch faded away.

The night was not over. Another disturbance began at 3:00 A.M. The family had come to fear this hour, sometimes called the "high noon of the demonic day." It started when Arne Johnson walked into the living room and tripped over an invisible obstacle; he fell to the floor with a loud crash. The noise woke up David. A few seconds later, a sofa cushion was observed to be pressed down, as though someone was sitting on it. According to David, now speaking lucidly as himself, the beast had just sat down.

In response, David got off the sofa and headed for

the kitchen, but then suddenly backed off. He said the helper with the knife in its heart was in the doorway, and the other entities were also in the room. Moments later, David was pushed onto his back.

Debbie's journal tells what happened:

David was lying on the living room floor. His body started rocking from side to side. Then his legs started to move up and down. I hung on to David's legs, and I started to go up and down with his legs. I couldn't get it to stop, so Alan hopped on with me, and it moved both of us. Between the two of us we weighed 295 pounds. And still David's legs kept moving us back and forth. Then this figure stomped on David's back, so mom had to use holy water on him, which worked but took some effort to do it.

The horrendous events of the night stopped only as darkness gave way to dawn. At noon, an unhappy Pat Giddings called. Her dog, Cha-Chi, had been found on the road in front of her house. The animal's whole back had been smashed. It would never walk again, said the veterinarian, and would probably die. It was the fulfillment of a prediction made only days before.

"The beast said he did it," David declared the moment Judy hung up the phone. "The beast was laughing all the time you were talking, and then he told me that he picked up Cha-Chi and threw him under the wheels of a car driving by to punish Mrs. Giddings for helping us."

Another day had started. It would not end any better. That afternoon, Judy took David to see a psychiatrist. Regrettably, the lengthy trip was useless, as Judy related:

"After all the terrible things we'd been through with David, I had my hopes built up that this doctor might help us. If he could explain what was wrong with David from a medical standpoint, fine. All I wanted was an *end* to the problem. You can't imagine what we were living through!

"When we got to his office, no-smoking signs were hanging all over, but the doctor had pipes everywhere you looked. Then he couldn't remember David's name, and fumbled around forever looking for a slip of paper where he had my son's name written down. Pathetic!

"While we were there, David was fine. He was himself, and when he's himself, you couldn't ask for a better kid. The doctor asked David a bunch of questions like—what was his favorite thing to do, what was his favorite color, and did he like his father. Then he had David tell him about the beast and especially all the things that were being done to him. The doctor kept saying, 'Oh really?' in this artificial way. From what I could gather, he seemed to think *we* were beating David, because of the bruises all over his body.

"After that, he had David draw a picture of the beast, which David did poorly. Then he finally showed David a bunch of ink blots, asking 'Does this look like the devil? How about this one? Or this one?' And David answering that they looked like butterflies, or parachutes, or a duck's behind. In the end I was told David was fine. There was nothing at all wrong with him. Everything the kid went through didn't happen. The welts didn't exist. Instead, *we* should all come back later in the week and start family therapy. Then he slapped a bill on me for seventy dollars. And I brought twenty along, just in case the visit got expensive! We were made fools of, just like the entity said would happen. It was hopeless."

"That doctor should have been in the car with us when we were going home," Alan added. "David told us the beast was riding in the backseat, and that all the helpers were riding up on the roof. The speedometer went crazy when we passed a funeral home down by the Warrens' house. And the helpers picked up the whole back end of my mom's station wagon. She was fighting to keep on the road—we were sitting up on an angle with only the front wheels touching down! Boy, were people looking at us! And when we got to the toll booth, the helpers picked up the *whole* car and drifted us five feet ahead when my mom stuck her hand out to give the guy money. He told us to just go ahead."

The following day, August 13, 1980, was a special occasion to the Glatzel family. But the torment didn't stop. A beautifully decorated cake was ruined; sounds of breaking glass and creaking boards echoed through the house; and David was subjected to a double dose of physical abuse.

They made his body bounce up and down for half an hour. Often his body was bounced so quickly that the movements couldn't be counted. Though David yelled pitifully for help, no one could stop it.

"Why? Dear God, why tonight?" Judy cried in anguish.

David was twelve now. The ruined cake was his. That day was his birthday.

Chapter XVIII

"Mr. Johnson? Father will see you now. Please come with me."

It was cool and quiet in the Retreat house in Stamford. Arne Johnson followed the white-robed nun down the hallway and into a book-filled office.

"Father Virgulak, this is Mr. Johnson," she said, then closed the door and walked away.

The Catholic priest, a man in his late thirties, greeted Arne with a handshake and restrained smile, then offered him a chair. Arne knew nothing about Father Virgulak, except that he exuded an air of competence.

The data pertaining to the possession of David Glatzel, submitted to the chancery offices by the priests in Brookfield, had been reviewed during the week, and responsibility for the case had been delegated to Father Francis Virgulak, who was both theological adviser to the bishop and theologian for the diocese. Along with his clerical functions at the diocese, he was director of the program on charismatic renewal—an esoteric branch of theology concerned with spiritual guidance and problems of mystical import.

Originally, Judy, David, and Arne were to have met with Father Virgulak, in the hope that some resolution to the case—perhaps through the laying-on-of-hands technique—could be effected that day. However, getting David into a religious building was out of the question. Arne apologized for David's absence. The priest understood the problem. At the same time, he also wanted to speak with Arne—because Arne had challenged the diabolical spirit in the boy. The Warrens had also recommended him as being the best spokesman on the case.

On the drive down from Brookfield, Debbie was pessimistic. She was sure no one would believe what was happening to her brother.

But, as Arne discovered, that was hardly the case. Father Virgulak was well versed on the subject of demonology, and he and Arne talked for two hours. The priest was concerned primarily with David's appearance and voice pattern under possession, and the kinds of things the entity said when it spoke.

Having thoroughly questioned Arne, the priest finally assured him that the Church had time-tested procedures for dealing with demonic possession, and that what they were experiencing was in fact nothing new.

When their discussion was finished, Father Virgulak imparted a blessing on Arne, then gave him a silver crucifix to wear around his neck, holy salts to use on David; and a statue of the Madonna to place in the home.

"One thing that struck me as being odd," Arne later recalled, "was that during the blessing my head was bowed and my eyes were closed, but I could *feel*

188

the movements of Father Virgulak's hand above my head, although he never touched me at all."

Upon leaving, the priest encouraged Arne to remain vigilant, and said that he would take positive steps in the next few days to put an end to the trouble and free David from possession.

Driving back to Brookfield, Arne told Debbie the details of the interview. For the first time since the case began, they had reason to feel hopeful and encouraged. Indeed, it was a doubly good day for Arne and Debbie. That morning Arne had at last secured a full-time job as a tree surgeon in Bethel, about ten miles from Brookfield. The day was Friday, August 15, 1980.

Arne and Debbie communicated their optimism to the family at dinner that night. But their positive mood was soon destroyed. The beast intensified its possession of David, and, perhaps of greater consequence, it began plaguing Father Virgulak.

Throughout that entire weekend, David was almost constantly under possession, his body used alternately as a target for physical torture and as a vehicle for the beast to speak and act through, this time reaching new lows of vulgarity.

David was not told that Father Virgulak gave Arne a silver cross to wear as a device of protection. But under possession he knew all about it.

"I don't want you wearing any damn cross from any damn priest, Johnson!" said the deep man's voice, speaking out of David's mouth. Backing up its declaration, the entity directed a piercing gaze at Arne's chest, whereupon the silver cross separated from the chain and, in full view of the family, whizzed across the room and struck Debbie in the forehead.

This phenomenon was repeated in other ways. Under possession, David could simply stare at an object

and cause it to careen across the room. A pen, a cigarette lighter, a toy truck—all became lethal weapons in
the proximity of the possessed child. "He could stare or
point at an object and suddenly it was in the air, coming straight at you," said Debbie. "We all got hit a
number of times until it became necessary to gather up
small objects and put them away in drawers, because
these things usually came flying at your head and had
the potential to put an eye out. And, of course, every
time we got hit, the beast laughed."

The new holy salts didn't work. Instead of stopping
attacks on David's body, they turned him—or that which
was in him—wild with pain. The bizarre wailing that
resulted was too much for the family to endure and the
salts were never used again.

The statue of the Madonna was useless. "It stood
about a foot high, all white, on a black base with a felt
bottom," Judy recalled. "It was a Madonna holding an
infant Jesus, and Arne put it on the fireplace mantel for
all our benefit. Well, when the beast was in David, it
got hold of that statue and turned it into a sex object. I
was forced to watch and listen to a shameful, depraved
situation with this thing manipulating the statue in a
grossly impure way, all the while saying in a deep
man's voice raw vulgarities like 'eat me' and 'f—— me'
and 'the Blessed Virgin is a f——ing whore.' This beast
thing was a sickening, lusting pervert—among other
things. It spoke about sexual degradations most adults
never even heard of. Sin and vice and lust and death
and hatred of God is all it ever talked about, once it got
going. I was constantly sick to my stomach."

When David was not in the throes of overt possession, he talked lucidly about the comings and goings
of the beast and its forty-odd helpers. When a rational

conversation could be held with the boy, one of the first questions asked was: Where are they?

Typically David would answer, "The beast is at Mary's; the one eyed helper is in the bedroom; number thirty-six is on the roof; the two chief helpers are at the Warrens'; the burned one is in the basement. . . ."

However, now the answer changed. When asked where the entities were, David invariably replied, "The beast and all the helpers are with Father Virgulak at the chancery."

When asked why they were there, David's response was always: "To stop the exorcism."

As extreme as David's statements sounded, and as eager as the Glatzels were to deny their content, they also knew that whatever the child said almost always proved true. Thus, the idea that this infernal thing might stop the plans for an exorcism—the family's one last hope—filled them with doubt and despair.

"You have to understand," said Judy, "we never spoke about exorcism in front of David, for fear that he would come under even worse attack. He got *all* his information from the beast. When it came to Father Virgulak, only Arne had met him, yet David described the priest to a tee in terms of appearance, and he was able to describe with complete detail the interior of the priest's office and his personal chambers, without ever once having been there."

Whether David was asleep or awake, the possession and torment of his body continued. While he was sleeping, coarse voices issued from his mouth. They spoke of killing, death, and hell. Often, Arne, Debbie, Judy, and Alan would gather around David and recite prayers over him, in a vain attempt to persuade the possessing entities to leave.

A half-hour tape-recording made of one of these

desperate vigils, with Arne leading the prayers, reveals an outpouring of concern and affection for David. Declarations of "We love you, David" and "Jesus repels you from this child" are interspersed with the sounds of gagging, slaps, and gasps of pain coming from the sleeping boy.

The Warrens documented the ghastly manipulations of David's body even while he was asleep. "Lorraine and I saw David's body bloated up to deadly proportions by these forces. His head swelled up to the size of a basketball. His abdomen ballooned to three times its normal size, as did his arms and legs and even his fingers. The bloating was severe to the degree that David's body could not expand any more, and cracks developed in his skin from the swelling. It looked like David was going to *explode*."

It is no surprise, therefore, that these late-night sessions, which started off as prayer readings, frequently turned into amateur attempts at exorcism. Arne Johnson, overwhelmed by David's unceasing misery, responded not with shock or rage but with *compassion* for the sufferings of his young friend.

On the night of August 16, with tears in his eyes, Arne leaned over and placed the silver cross given to him by Father Virgulak on David's forehead and said, "In the name of Jesus Christ, leave David's body! Come out of him and take me on. I'm stronger than David. I'll fight you. Leave David and *come into me!*"

The cross left a momentary impression on David's forehead, but Arne's statement would endure. Arne Johnson would be made to pay for this spontaneous, Christ-like gesture. The penalty would come due not that day or that weekend, but in exactly six months to the date, at 6:06 P.M. At that time, Arne Johnson's life would become a living death.

On Sunday, August 17, Father Francis Virgulak drove up from Stamford to confer with the Warrens on what was then called the Brookfield Possession Case. He explained that he was going to serve as theologian on the case, which pleased the Warrens. They had known and admired Father Frank, as they called him, since 1972, when he worked with them on the successful exorcism of a home near Hartford, on a street ironically named Beelzebub Avenue.

The objective of that conference at the Warrens' home was to devise an exorcism strategy. "There were two schools of thought," said Ed Warren. "As far as I was concerned, we were dealing with a clear-cut case of diabolic possession. All the stages had occurred; they'd occurred in the right order; and we had rock-solid evidence to justify the validity of the phenomena at each stage—along with three priests to back up everything. It was all laid out on a silver platter, and to me, given the cruelty and violence taking place in the home, the best and quickest solution was to conduct major exorcism and be done with it.

"Father Virgulak, on the other hand, wanted to go the conservative route and start with lesser exorcism, then move *up to* the Rituale Romanum, if it was needed. Instead of formally expelling the entities, his idea was to use charismatic procedures, in which the positive power of God is substituted or implanted in the home to displace the negative power of the devil. Light would replace darkness. He suggested this could best be done by performing a High Mass inside the Glatzel house. Father Virgulak offered to serve as chief celebrant of the Mass, and seemed to have his mind set on this approach, so we agreed to support him. The Mass was set for Wednesday, August twentieth. The intervening three days were needed for preparation."

After six weeks of continuous crisis, the Glatzels were now going to get help. A Mass was a far more desirable solution to them, compared to the horrific thought of exorcism. Between August 17 and 20, the family thus invested all their hope in the belief that the High Mass would solve the problem. But the warnings made by the beast tempered their enthusiasm. Once again it declared that there would be no exorcism and it would drive away the priests.

"You are the Father of Lies," Arne told it that Sunday night. "We don't believe you. We'll all fight against you until the very end. You can be sure of that. We won't stop until you're gone!"

"If you get in my way I'll ruin your life," the beast threatened, speaking through David's mouth.

Despite the entity's threats that it would not allow a Mass to be performed in the home, the High Mass began as planned, on Wednesday, August 20, at three o'clock in the afternoon.

Father Virgulak was chief celebrant; Father Grosso, Father Millea, and Father DiGiovanni were concelebrants. The Mass was the culmination of long, diligent hours of preparation. Approval for the Mass had to be obtained from the chancery; a correct liturgy had to be researched and selected; days of prayer had to be performed by the priests involved.

This preparation was apparently not done without some harassment of the clergy by the beast. "Don't stay alone. Don't travel alone. Sleep with someone else in the room at night," Father Virgulak privately directed the three other priests before the Mass began.

A long wooden table functioned as an altar. An altar cloth was brought from the Brookfield church and draped over the table. Church candles were set up, as were gold chalices and cut-glass cruets filled with wine, water, and holy oils. A historic cross that came from the original St. Jopseph's Church in Brookfield was placed in the center of the Altar.

Attending the Mass were Carl and Judy Glatzel, Carl, Jr., Debbie, Alan, David, Arne Johnson, and Ed and Lorraine Warren. All were dressed in their Sunday best. Jason stayed next door with Pat Giddings, in case trouble occurred.

"David was well behaved," remembers Ed Warren. "Possession had typically been inflicted on him each night before the Mass, but that afternoon he seemed clear. Still, he paced nervously from room to room before the priests got started, eyeing the altar every once in a while. I was concerned he might go under, and turn the whole place upside down, but he behaved just fine.

"Young Carl is the one who bolted. About five minutes before we were supposed to get under way, Carl became very hostile. 'I'm getting out of here, I don't need this,' he said. 'You're not getting me in that living room; if I want to go to Mass I'll do it in a church!' Then he tore off his tie, ran outside, and never came back."

The family moved to the living room and took seats. David sat on the couch between his father and Ed Warren. After consecrating the altar with incense, the priests, dressed in full vestments of purple (symbolic of mourning), began the High Mass.

About ten minutes into the proceedings, David suddenly started gagging. Father Virgulak looked up from the altar and made the sign of the cross in front of David. The attack stopped immediately.

The ceremony continued with the reading of a prayer for the deliverance from evil in place of a homily, then moved on toward Communion. Once again trouble threatened, as a growling issued from David's body.

Father Virgulak cast holy water on the boy with an aspergillum, and once again there was quiet.

Those who were prepared to receive it took Communion. Additional prayers were read, imploring the intervention of Jesus, and asking for David and the family to be released from bondage to the forces of darkness. Lastly, David was blessed with holy oils. By four o'clock the High Mass had been completed.

"It was as though the heavy, dense atmosphere had been lifted," said Lorraine Warren. "There was a difference. We all felt it. I could report to Father Virgulak at the end that there were no spirit forces in the house. But that didn't mean the entities were expelled. It only meant they had withdrawn. No one could predict whether the invading spirits would respect the aura of holiness implanted in the house by the High Mass, or defy it and return. Only time would tell."

Nevertheless, all *seemed* fine after the High Mass. Photographs were taken of David, holding a cross in front of the altar, smiling freely as himself.

But would it last?

Chapter XIX

Calm replaced chaos in the Glatzel house after the High Mass on August 20. David was no longer possessed, and all the bizarre phenomena came to an immediate halt. When the Warrens visited the Glatzels that weekend, all they heard was good news. In three days there had not been one unnatural incident. David so appreciated his newfound freedom that he bought the Warrens a present with some of his birthday money. It was a small ceramic duck, which he wrapped himself. Attached to the gift was a handwritten card that said, "Thank you for everything. David."

Despite the atmosphere of hope and optimism, the essential question remained: Was it really over? Or was this simply a deceptive lull? A seven-day waiting period was in effect.

"One permanent result of conducting the Mass in the Glatzel house," said Ed Warren, "was that there were no more bangings on the wall, or explosions, or the levitation of large objects. Ninety-nine percent of the gross manipulations of the physical environment came to a stop. We knew, from experience, that if lesser demonic entities were responsible for the havoc, then the Mass could potentially suffice as a form of exorcism. But if higher *diabolical* forces were involved, then they would only obey the commands imposed on them through a formal exorcism. In such a case, the entities would back off and the siege would stop for a few days; but activity would then come roaring back with twice the ferocity."

What happened during that seven-day watch period?

The activity came back—with vehemence! By the end of the week, David was fully under possession again.

The relapse began surreptitiously; in fact, it did not even begin in the Glatzel house. It began next door, in the home of their neighbor, Pat Giddings, who received a bizarre, obscene phone call.

"No one could see into my bedroom, even if they tried," said Pat. "On Monday morning, about quarter to nine, the telephone rang on my nightstand. The shades were down and the drapes were closed. I was in my nightgown. I'd been up five minutes and hadn't left the room. But this voice, in a deep, husky whisper, said it was with me and could see me. To prove itself, it described exactly what I had on, right down to the color of the underwear under my robe and nightgown. Then it continued and said things like, *'I want your body! I'm gonna get your body!'* It didn't stop there, but instead reeled off all kinds of sexually perverted things it proposed to do. When I asked, 'Who is this?' the voice answered in a hostile, demanding tone: *'Don't help the Glatzels!'* The call scared me so much that I hung up and phoned the Brookfield Police Department and told them what happened. They sent a policewoman over, and I wouldn't let her leave until I was fully dressed. I was frightened for my life."

Pat Giddings was not alone. At the rectory, an equally threatening call was made to the priests that same night. The voice on the line told them to "stay the Goddamn hell out of my house!" the call evoked considerable confusion, because the voice on the other end of the line *sounded like* Carl Glatzel, Sr. But it was not.

And there were other calls. After it rang peculiarly, Alan answered the Glatzels' phone, and a coarse man's voice told him that he'd be stabbed, through David. At that time, other people in Brookfield—people who had nothing to do with the case—reported receiving similar vulgar calls.

But the real renewal of the seige occurred when David began hearing the cry of a young girl calling out in the distance, *"Help me, David!"* Then, as he slept, a strained voice spoke through him and said, *"Beware! Arne dies at work tomorrow!"* Alan got the statement on tape.

The following day, Arne, who was enjoying his new job as a tree surgeon, was working one hundred feet up an elm tree when his rigging suddenly let go. In seconds he dropped seventy feet through the branches until his pulley gear checked the fall. "You should have been killed," Arne's foreman told him afterward.

No less dangerous was a situation that occurred in downtown Bethel. David had been confined to the house for over a month, and they felt it was now safe to take him out for a ride when they went shopping.

"We were sitting at a stop light in the center of town," said Debbie, "with Alan, Jason, and Arne in the backseat, and my mother and David in the front. Suddenly David got fidgety and had a faraway look in his eyes. The next thing I knew, he grabbed the steering wheel and stomped on the gas pedal. In seconds we were careening full speed down Main Street. Arne had to immediately grab the steering wheel too, and I slammed on the brakes. I could hardly overcome David's strength, because his foot was squashing my right foot on the accelerator, while I was trying to brake with my left. Luckily, we stopped only moments before we were about to hit a group of people in an intersection. After it happened, the thing in David laughed, in the deep man's voice. That's when we knew it wasn't over."

That Sunday night, outbreaks of phenomena returned. Humming vibrations were heard in the house; square flashing lights appeared on the walls of darkened rooms; the beast's head was superimposed over the faces of family members in framed pictures; an empty, unconnected washing machine unaccountably flooded the basement; and spirit forms appeared, many of them wearing shrouds.

By Monday, August 25, David was back under bouts of full possession. The first statement the entity made after taking over David's body was directed at Arne: *"I'm going to kill you, and the next time I won't fail!"*

But that's not all the possessing entity said. Enraged about the High Mass, it told them off—in an odd, mystical language that none of them could understand. "We have a familiarity with Italian, Dutch, and Slavic in our family," said Judy, "but this was a totally different language, a weird one, that sounded like no human language I ever heard."

It seemed as if all the stops had been pulled. In response to prayers said in its presence, the possessing entity in the child would make the sign of the cross backward, and scream, *"Our Father Who art in Hell, this soul belongs to Satan!"*

200

Attacks on David's body regained their severity. He was stabbed, shot, and clubbed. One night the beast made David's body do sit-ups for almost an hour. After that, the beast left David's body, and the boy vomited.

When the entity wasn't alternately possessing David's body for hours at a time, it used him to furiously attack the other members of the family. Under possession, the child would wait, with knives and fireplace pokers, for an opportune moment to strike. Wild, surreal scenes of violence would then unfold in the house. Someone's life was always in jeopardy. At one point, Arne grabbed David's wrist just in time to prevent a murder: David had been about to stab Alan in the stomach with a steak knife. Enraged, the entity screamed, *"I'll possess you for that!"*

And indeed it did possess Arne. As Debbie explained, "That night after the knife incident, Arne was sitting with my parents and me at the kitchen table. Suddenly, out of nowhere, he started to go through these ugly convulsions like David used to get when he first came under possession. When the shaking was over, Arne's face was distorted-looking, and his features were drawn back, bony-like, into an animal sneer. His eyes were glassy and wild. Then a growling sound came out of him. 'Oh my God,' I said, 'now it's happening to Arne!' "

The possession of Arne lasted less than a minute. However, it was only the first of six possession episodes, of which the last would result in tragedy. The phenomena, meanwhile, continued in the most outrageous manner. One particularly stunning incident concerned what Debbie called "the claw":

"During the night, while I was lying on my sleeping bag, I'd sometimes feel a cold hand touch me. In the morning I'd often have scratches on me that weren't there when I went to bed. One night in late August I felt movement by my arm. I reached down and touched something really cold and scaly. When I opened my eyes to look, it was gone. The next night the same thing happened, but this time a light was on and I *saw* it. There was a big, scaly, green-gray claw sticking up *through* the floor. It had three clawlike fingers with a nail at the end of each one. Before I could do anything, this lizard claw ran its nails down the side of my arm and scratched it in three wiggly lines. Then the claw went back down through the floor. This didn't happen once—it happened a number of times. Arne saw the claw too; he also had odd scratches on his chest. David said the claw belonged to number 40. Number 40 was an eight-foot tall ghoul that was supposed to guard the basement."

New, highly intensive phenomena and deeper, more intensified possession characterized this relapse phase. And though the same entity, the beast, came through David as before, it now exhibited an intelligence never seen before under all the crudity. Typical was the response given to Judy when she told the beast, "The priests are going to exorcize you, and then you will have to obey the commands of God!"

"Never! I will never obey the commands of God; I will never be exorcized! It is 'Better to reign in hell, than serve in heaven'!" the entity declared, quoting Milton's *Paradise Lost*, Book I, line 263.

This resurgence of possession and phenomena made it obvious that genuine exorcism was needed. Therefore, a week after the High Mass, Father Virgulak and the Warrens conferred again. Father Virgulak had already consulted with the other priests in Brookfield and was in the process of making a recommendation of action to the bishop.

"Given the gravity of matters," said Ed Warren, "Father Virgulak felt there should be no more stalling. Attempts at lesser exorcism would be fruitless. There was an overwhelming need for major exorcism, and his recommendation was that the Rituale Romanum be said over the boy as soon as possible. But this could only happen if the case fulfilled the criteria laid down by the Church:

"Has the individual divulged hidden or future knowledge?

"Has the individual spoken in unorthodox tongues, or in languages previously unknown to him?

"Has the individual demonstrated preternatural powers, or caused actions distinctly beyond the bounds of human ability?

"Has the possessing entity identified itself by name, or else given some indisputable sign of a diabolical presence?

" 'Yes' was the answer to every question," Ed declared. "David was a regular oracle, and we had many of his predictions on tape. In terms of languages, I'd heard him talk forward in three different voices than his own, as well as one time talking *backwards*. In addition to speaking English in an extraordinarily high and extraordinarily low vocabulary, it also spoke a 'magic tongue,' knew Latin, and even quoted verse. David's ability to see through walls demonstrated preternatural powers, while the bouncings and bloatings of his body indicated actions beyond human ability—on the physical side. As for a distinguishing sign, the entity *called* itself Satan, but it hadn't yet truly divulged its name; out of pride, however, it had branded its likeness on David's leg in a vivid red patch. The case fulfilled all four points established by the Church—although only one point had to be met in order to justify the need for major exorcism. There was no deviation from canon law.

"All the time we were talking with Father Frank," Ed recalls, "the Glatzels kept calling us, giving updated developments. I felt like directing the calls to the bishop's office, where they should have gone. After six weeks of crisis and torment, including a full-fledged case of diabolical possession, the only person in authority to set foot in the Glatzel house from the Diocese of Bridgeport was Father Virgulak, on the day of the High Mass. I considered that highly indifferent and certainly no way to uphold the word of Christ. I started to get the sinking feeling that a tragedy was brewing. The case was not being managed correctly. Nevertheless, when Father Virgulak left our house that afternoon, he had all the necessary data to request exorcism under the basis of canon law. He took the tapes and photographs with him to submit as additional evidence. If that didn't do it, then something was wrong, very wrong."

In his discussion with the Warrens, Father Virgulak alluded to "sudden difficulties" the clergy were having because of their involvement in the case: uncanny phenomena were being directed at the priests, while others—including Father Virgulak—were being subjected to visitations from entities in black. The need and the desire for a major exorcism was obvious.

Two days later, Father Virgulak called the Warrens and informed them that the decision had been made to exorcize David. After consulting with the priests in Brookfield, the "deliverance" was set for Tuesday, September 2, in the school chapel at St. Joseph's.

The word *deliverance*, the Warrens were astounded to learn, meant that the bishop had refused permission for the Rituale Romanum! True exorcism would be attempted, but using a different liturgy, or rite, to accomplish the task.

Lorraine Warren explains, "To prepare for this grave procedure, the priests dedicated Low Masses during the week for the successful release of the child; they engaged in three days of prayer and fasting ["Some spirits can be cast out in no way except by prayer and fasting." St. Mark, IX.]; and they asked their congregations to say additional prayers for an unnamed special intention. The latter point developed into a huge prayer network up and down the East coast by the weekend of August thirtieth."

For the Glatzels, what mattered most was that exorcism was going to take place. It *had* to take place: their lives were in shambles, and they couldn't bear it any longer.

On Tuesday, September 2, a classic exorcism took place in Brookfield Center.

The site of the exorcism was the altar of St. Joseph's school chapel. At one o'clock, Father Virgulak arrived at the school and met with Fathers Grosso, Millea, and DiGiovanni. Father Virgulak would be the exorcist; the three other priests would carry out specific functions as his assistants. It was a serious moment in the lives of all four priests, and after talking they repaired to the chapel to pray.

"For days, David was completely out of control," says Ed Warren, "and as the exorcism date drew closer, his behavior grew worse. When Lorraine and I arrived at the Glatzel's house at one-thirty that afternoon to take the family to the church, David was fully under possession, and holding his grandmother—who was visiting from out of state—at *knifepoint*.

"The possessing entity was speaking through David

and went into an abusive rampage when it saw us, threatening me and showering Lorraine with vulgarities. David's father took advantage of the distraction, grabbing his son's wrist and wrestling the knife from him. A few seconds later, growling and spitting and biting, the entity in David attacked everyone. To get David to the church, we had to tackle, subdue, and tie him into a chair with sheets."

Although the body of the child was bound, the entity was not. It continued to speak and shout. David's lips never moved, his eyes never blinked, his muscles never flexed, but flaming threats and accusations continued to pour out of his body in a husky man's voice:

"You'll never cast me out! You bastards will never win! The priests will go! I'll never obey! You're all shit for hell!"

"Mommy, please, untie my arms. Please, mommy, the sheets hurt."

"I'll get you!"

"You win! Let me free! I'll give you what you want!"

"You'll be sorry for this! All yours hands will be full!"

It was this uncontrollable fury, this dynamo of evil, that broke the monastic quiet of the school chapel that Tuesday afternoon at two o'clock. David was under possession, and that which possessed him was maniacally enraged. Now untied, David was forcibly ushered into the chapel by his father and Ed Warren. The strength the boy exerted under possession was enormous.

David was brought to a pew in the front row, where the four priests stood waiting. The priests were dressed in black day clothes, over which was worn a white surplice and purple stole—the prescribed dress. Both Carl and Judy Glatzel were present, as were Debbie, Arne, and Alan. Carl, Jr., refused to come, while Debbie's son, Jason, stayed home with the grandmother—who'd known nothing about the case, and was now shocked and terrified.

The Warrens attended in a professional capacity. Lorraine's task was to discern the presence and nature of entities. Ed was present to lend expertise as a demonologist; he would protect the priests, guide the proceedings, and make sure the exorcism rite was completed, no matter what happened.

The planned ritual consisted of first anointing all the individuals with holy oils for protection; then a reading of prayers and psalms; the discernment of entities; the casting out of those entities by the exorcist; and last, a final blessing of thanksgiving for the release of a "mortal soul from bondage to the Eternal Enemy." Theoretically, the rite was a peaceful one. If a ruckus ensued, humans would not be the cause of it.

The anointing with oils proceeded without incident. The reading of preliminary prayers came next:

> In the Name of Jesus Christ, our Lord and Saviour, strengthened by the intercession of the Immaculate Virgin, Mother of God, of the Blessed Michael, the Archangel, of the Blessed Apostles and all the Saints, we undertake to repulse the attacks and deceits of the devil.

But the possessing entity in David did not let a statement go by without a vulgar rebuttal: *"Jesus is —— . . . Mary is a ——." . . . .*

By the end of the introductory prayer, David broke loose from Ed Warren's grasp and sought to attack the priests physically. The possessed child was caught, restrained, and brought back to the pew, snorting and growling and struggling.

The reading continued:

Let God arise, let his enemies be scattered; let them that hate the Lord Almighty flee before Him. As smoke is driven away so let the wicked perish at the presence of God.

Shut up, you pious fool! You bunch of mother-fuckers! You foul swine! You . . ."

"Silence!" Father Virgulak demanded.

"Did you like it when I blew out your light bulb? . . . Hahahahaheeee . . ."

The priest was astonished. A few nights earlier, the bulb in Father Virgulak's desk lamp had inexplicably exploded, showering him with bits of glass.

"Silence!" Father Grosso demanded.

"Don't you dare command me! You ape! You swine! You fucking slob! This is for you!"

Father Grosso suddenly flinched. The entity had projected a slash, and when the priest pulled up his pant cuff, blood was running down his leg.

Father Virgulak continued reading the prayers above the shouts and catcalls of the possessing entity. Failing at verbal disruption, David got loose again and was pinned down at the foot of the altar. After nearly an hour, the boy still exhibited inexhaustible strength and indefatigable resistance to the exorcism.

Ed, Arne, and Alan held David at the foot of the altar, as Father Virgulak then began reading the commands of exorcism:

Behold the Cross of the Lord, flee bands of enemies. We drive you from us, whoever you may be, unclean spirits. Satanic powers, infernal invaders, wicked legions; in the Name and by the Virtue of Our Lord Jesus Christ depart from this Lamb of God.

The entity in David, however, turned wild. It spit profusely all over Father Virgulak, Father Grosso, and Ed Warren. It bit and cursed and shrieked and howled. Blasphemies and profanities echoed unceasingly around the church. Fortunately, the doors were all securely locked.

Father Virgulak returned again and again to the commands of exorcism. The entity, in opposition, responded with a litany of sins it accused the others of committing, while accusing the priests of engaging in every kind of sexual perversity imaginable. The thing named members of the priests' families and threatened to attack them in retaliation.

Despite the wearying abuse and torrents of lies, and invectives, the exorcism commands were continued:

Begone Satan! Cease your audacity. Withdraw from the elect of God. Cease your malice. Cease your insolence. Stay your perditious iniquity. This is the command made to you by the Most High God! God the Father commands you; God the Son commands you; God the Holy Ghost commands you! I command you, in the name of the God Almighty, the Creator to produce the sign of thine departure and begone from the world redeemed by the Precious Blood of our Lord Jesus Christ.

An awful groan issued from David's body. Momentarily, thereafter, the pages of hymnbooks were heard rustling in the back of the church; then the sound of footsteps; then, lastly, the opening and closing of a door.

A sign had been given. Now Lorraine Warren's gift of discernment was critical.

Her response: "All the lesser spirits are gone. They've quit. They're expelled."

Staring at the pitiful spectacle of the possessed boy who lay gasping on the carpet at the foot of the altar, Lorraine continued with the discernment process:

"Four spirits remain in the child now. These are the strongest . . . they have orchestrated it all . . . but one . . . only one of them is the power.

"Gluttony is present . . . Lust is present . . . a high entity using the name Gaytois is present . . . but deep, off in the distance, is the final one . . . it is the power. The first three are demonic. The last one . . . the one that has done all this . . . the one responsible . . . that one, Father, is a devil!"

Screaming and yelling erupted out of David the moment Lorraine uttered the last syllable.

"You'll never expel me!" the lead voice declared. *"He is mine! His soul is mine! It is mine!"*

If the first hour of the exorcism was a battle, the second was a war. Virtually everyone was covered with spit and slobber, particularly the priests. All were kicked and punched and bitten. All were forced to endure lying accusations and were repulsed by monumentally depraved blasphemies against Christ, Mary, and the Church.

In the middle of the screaming, Father Grosso whispered to Lorraine that a large folding knife appeared to be in David's shirt pocket. Although Lorraine barely heard the priest, the very next statement from the possessing entity was: *"The knife is mine and I know what to do with it!"*

What had obviously been a physical object in the boy's pocket disappeared when Ed Warren reached for it. His efforts were met with raucous laughter from the beast.

What possessed David was overwhelming in power and strength, and it used everything it had to stop the exorcism, including deception.

As the priest continued with the commands of exorcism, David began to talk as himself:

"Please, mommy. Please. Everybody's hurting me. I just want to get out of here. I don't want to stay here, mommy. Make them stop hurting me. I want to get out of this church. Mommy, please, I'll be good. I promise. I just want to get out of this church."

The pleading was sufficiently deceptive to prompt Father Virgulak to bend down and speak to the boy, whereupon his stole was suddenly grabbed by the thing in the child, who began strangling him. The priest did not make that mistake again.

Two hours into the exorcism, the entity began causing disfigurements of David's body. He was bloated and bounced and choked nearly to death.

"Please, mommy! They're killing me! Make them stop! Are you there, mommy? Get me out of here before they kill me!"

David's face had turned blue. His eyes and tongue protruded grossly. But Father Virgulak persisted in the commands of expulsion. Long, tortured animal wails sounded from David's body at the very same time he was gagging.

Father Virgulak looked down at the grotesque scene and stepped back. The bulging eyes were crazed and wild. The tongue was so swollen that air could not be drawn. The devil really was the antithesis of life. It *would* kill.

211

For the clergy, this was the critical point. They were involved in an enormous game of chance on a high mystical level. If they continued, the boy would either be exorcized or in minutes he would die.

At four o'clock that Tuesday afternoon Father Virgulak stopped the exorcism. He could not risk David's death. Making the sign of the cross over the restrained boy, he declared, *"Dominus Vobiscum."*

Expectedly, the fury subsided at that point. The entity, at least for the time being, had won. David Glatzel remained possessed.

Yet, all was not lost: the legion of lesser possessing entities was now gone from the child, never to appear again. Testament to that fact was found in the back of the church, where hymnbooks were scattered all over the floor.

Still, the four main entities remained. As Debbie Glatzel's journal entry for the night of September 2 indicates:

> 9:45 P.M.: David went into a trancelike state and started fighting with us hard. Also spitting. He kicked over two bottles of holy water, and hit me in the jaw with a book when I wasn't paying attention and hurt me. Then, on his stomach in the living room, we found David bobbing up and down. After that Carl [Jr.] and I saw David get knocked right over, backwards, and he started crying. He said the thing kicked him in the stomach. David was in a great deal of pain.

The outcome of the September 2 attempt at exorcism: the presiding entities were not dislodged. Further exorcism was called for.

Chapter XX

The days following the September 2 exorcism attempt were filled with enormous tension and difficulty. A solution had not been reached. Sanity and order had not been restored. David was still possessed.

However, the frequency and duration of each possession episode, as well as the number of brute physical attacks, were effectively reduced by half. This, at least, was a positive sign.

On the negative side, the forty-odd entities that had formerly participated in the seizure had not left entirely. The effect of exorcism was only to remove them from the child's body. David reported that they were still in the room with him.

Yet, as Ed Warren explained, the scope of the problem now extended beyond possession. "After the September second exorcism attempt, a backlash of intimidating phenomena was directed at all of us, including the clergy. Imagine waking up to find your bed pillow soaked with blood! That's what happened to one of the priests. 'The blood squished when I turned my head. It was all over my face,' he told us. The beast entity, in black form, repeatedly confronted another of the priests. The clergy suffered intense, driving head-aches; one began to lose his speaking voice; another was so upset that he was put on medication. The priests were never left alone."

But the gravity of the case went far deeper. Danger was brewing in the Glatzel home—long-term danger. The focus of that danger, the one threatened *by name*, was Arne Cheyenne Johnson.

Arne had remained steadfast. The priests and the Warrens came and went, but Arne never once conceded a point to the devil in David. For his dogged resistance, Arne suffered the full wrath and fury of the ruinous, diabolical thing.

"I will possess you," Arne was told during the week.

Accordingly, at Mass that Sunday, Arne was possessed again.

"I was sitting with Debbie, Jason, and the Glatzels," recalls Arne. "While the Mass was going on, I couldn't believe my eyes. One of the spirits I had seen—all black, with arms and legs—was on the altar with the priest while he was doing the ceremony. It was mimicking the priest's actions behind him. The next thing I knew, I was standing outside of church with Debbie, who was asking me why I did it. I didn't know what she was talking about."

"Arne was sitting quietly, with the rest of us in the pew," says Debbie, "Right at the point where the Host was raised up in the air, Arne started cursing—or I should say something started cursing through him, because his jaw was cracked open but his mouth didn't move. '*Son of a bitch . . . I want out of here. . . . Get me out of this f——ing goddamn church. . . .*'

"People immediately started turning around, but Arne wasn't in control. He seemed to be in a trance. After a few more choice things were said, I had to hustle him out the door. When I got Arne outside, I asked him, do you know what you just said in there? His answer was 'no.' Arne apologized all day long, but he never knew what happened to him. It was pathetic. The figure just made a fool out of Arne in front of the community."

This was the second episode of possession Arne had experienced. The incident might have been considered only a passing one, had it not been for an ominous prediction that came through David earlier in the week.

"I have come for a soul. I will take what is mine. I will possess Arne and kill with a knife."

The prediction did not stop there. The entity stated that Arne would be "caught for the crime." It then rattled off a series of names (which later turned out to be the lawyers and court officials in the legal case), finally declaring that Arne would be found guilty without a trial and be shut away for "life" in prison.

"I will ruin your life."

It meant it.

A second attempt to exorcise David was imperative. The date for this second exorcism was deliberately set for Monday, September 8, 1980. As Lorraine Warren explained, "We chose the eighth because we were hoping for a miracle. Many miraculous cures have occurred on September eighth, *including* sudden exorcisms. It is a day when possession does not occur, anywhere in the world. It is the Birthday of the Blessed Virgin Mary, the source of tremendous mystical power. We all believed that the case would either be won or lost on that date."

No trouble was expected, so the site of the exorcism was changed from the school chapel to the convent of St. Joseph's, a colonial building directly across from the Congregational Church.

The afternoon of September 8, while the other children of Brookfield were beginning a new school year, David Glatzel was brought to the convent house by his mother, his sister, and Alan. Waiting at the convent were the Warrens and the four priests.

Once everyone was settled, the doors were locked, the drapes were drawn, and David was seated in a large armchair. The objective—both simple and complex—was to read the rite of exorcism to the possessed child from beginning to end, without resistance or interference. The procedure was supposed to take an hour.

In the end, it took two hours. As anticipated, possession was not inflicted on David that day. He was fatigued but cooperative. The priests stood in a semicircle in front of the boy and began reading the prescribed introductory prayers. However, David told them immediately that the spirits were not present. They were at the house causing havoc. The proceedings were stopped and Ed Warren was dispatched to transfer the entities out of the Glatzel home.

"When I got to the house I found two of the Glatzels's relatives, older people, sitting wide-eyed in the kitchen," said Ed. "Just from the look of them I knew something had happened.

"I walked into the living room and the black rocking chair was going back and forth, full tilt. No one was sitting in it.

"I then walked down the hallway of the house and looked in each of the bedrooms. Everything seemed in

216

order, except in the Glatzels' master bedroom. The bed looked too high. When I took a second look, I saw it was levitating about six inches off the floor. I stepped into the room and immediately felt swamped by a sense of dread evil. Suddenly, the bed began to shake violently, the legs slamming onto the floor when they hit. It was shocking. The phenomenon lasted thirty seconds. It was a defiant show of force.

"Once the display of activity stopped, transferring the entities out of the house was basically a simple matter of placing a blessed object from the convent inside the Glatzel home. I put a small statue of St. Joseph on the mantel. After saying good-bye to the people in the kitchen, I drove back up to the convent house."

When Ed Warren returned, David reported that the spirits were all now in the convent. Strange thumps and movements of furniture, both in and above the day room, confirmed this. These unexpected diversions took a full hour to resolve.

Finally, at three o'clock, the exorcism began in earnest. It was the same lengthy reading attempted in the chapel on September 2. But the scene in the convent was drastically different from the previous one. This time there was no interference. The prayers and psalms were recited without interruption. There was no spitting, biting, cursing, or screaming.

Everyone waited for an interruption, if not a confrontation, but none arose. At four o'clock the final prayer of thanksgiving and beseechment was read aloud:

God of Heaven, God of Earth, God of Angels, God of Apostles, God who has power to give life after death and rest after work, we humbly beseech Thee to deliver us from all the tyranny of the infernal spirits, from their snares, and their furious wickedness. Deign, O Lord, to protect us by Thy power and to preserve us safe and sound. We beseech Thee through Jesus Christ our Lord. Amen.

Father Virgulak then rendered a formal blessing on David. It was over. The deed had been done.

What mattered now was the effect.

Would this stop possession of David? Would a miraculous end occur?

The answer would be known by midnight.

David's behavior was monitored from the moment he walked out of the convent. If the efforts of the afternoon were successful, there would be no more possession. The ultimate sign of termination would be for nothing to happen at all. Activity would stop. Forever.

After nine weeks of terror, David was racked and weary. He knew nothing about the horrific possession episodes that had besieged him; he only suffered the consequences. For David Glatzel, September 8 simply meant a day off from pain.

That night at the Glatzel house, those overseeing the case gathered to wait and watch. The Warrens had stayed with the family during the afternoon, and in the evening they were relieved by the priests from St. Joseph's.

At 10:30 P.M., Lorraine returned to the house, accompanied by Paul Bartz, one of Ed Warren's research assistants. For reasons of his own, Ed was not present that night. Shortly thereafter, Father Virgulak arrived.

Neither possession nor phenomena had occurred. David sat at the table, perfectly composed, drawing pictures of construction machinery. The contrast between David possessed and David normal was enormous.

At 11:30, David went into the living room and joined the other boys on the couch. All the religious ritual was over his head and he was getting tired.

"Wouldn't it be great if we just put David to bed tonight and in the morning it'd all be over," Debbie said. No one dared reply.

At midnight, all was well. David was holding his own. He was chattering with the others about fixing a hole in the stone wall in the yard. He was going to do this as soon as "the grownups made the beast go away."

Fifteen minutes later, David got up and started pacing. He no longer seemed tired. In fact, he was alert. When spoken to, his replies were brusque and sometimes nasty. It was consistent with behavior he displayed before coming under possession.

"David, why don't you go to bed," Judy suggested.

"I'm not tired!" he said sharply, returning to the living room, where his brothers and Arne were sitting with Paul Bartz. Paul, age thirty-three, has worked with the Warrens for almost a decade. His task tonight was to watch David. Should possession occur, Paul was to call Ed Warren immediately.

In the kitchen, more coffee was brewed and the wait continued. At 12:20 A.M., loud, boisterous talk erupted in the living room. Father Grosso, went in, sat down, and observed.

At 12:25, a paper airplane sailed across the room and hit Father Grosso in the chest. It came from David. When the priest looked at the boy, he was met with a burning stare.

Then, at 12:30, half an hour into September 9, the worst occurred. David came under possession.

219

The heartsinking alarm was raised by Paul Bartz: "He's going under!"

David's whole body began to vibrate. His eyes rolled up into his head, and moments later he was under.

"Leave!" the possessing entity screamed at the priests. David jumped to his feet, demanding in a vehement man's voice, *"Get out! You're not getting him!"*

A barrage of hostile accusations and vulgarities followed. The women were called sluts, whores, tramps, and prostitutes. The men were hit with insulting accusations of sexual misconduct; the priests were called queer. Father Virgulak, Lorraine Warren, and Judy Glatzel were threatened with death for going through with the exorcism.

Paul Bartz called Ed Warren. By the time Paul returned to the living room a minute later, David was utterly wild. Arne and Carl, Sr., were doing all they could to hold the boy back, as he struggled and strained to get at the priests, particularly Father Virgulak.

It had begun.

One by one the priests donned their purple stoles, determined to see this siege to an end.

With the strength David exhibited, it was a ten-minute battle just to get him down on the floor where he could be controlled. David's body was so imbued with force that four men were required to hold him down.

Father Virgulak traced a cross in the air; then, with the other priests beside him, he began the exorcism.

"I'm more powerful than God!"

"Silence!" Father Virgulak commanded, holding a small crucifix up to the boy. From his position on the floor David spat on the cross, ten feet away. *"You'll never exorcize me, you son of a bitching shithead!"*

Again Father Virgulak began the process by attempting to anoint David with holy oils. As he came toward David, the entity in the child broke out in insane laughter. *"That's the wrong oil, you holy fool!"*

The thing was right. The priest had inadvertently opened the wrong vial.

With the struggling, spitting, and biting, it took another ten minutes just to anoint David's forehead with the oils. Once applied, the holy oils trickled into David's mouth; he then spat it back into Father Virgulak's face.

Half an hour later, the physical struggle continued unabated. Alan and Carl, Jr., were called in to help.

Father Virgulak began reading the exorcism over the boy. But from the very first word, there was resistance. Virtually every word the priest said was met with a crude rebuttal, or just shouted down.

At 1:30 A.M. only the most minimal progress had been made. The mental and the physical resistance exerted by the possessing entity in the child was just as strong as it had been at the beginning. The struggle was constant. Just holding David down was a monumental task, while out of his mouth spewed a ferocious spate of humiliating and degrading lies about everyone present.

For the next thirty minutes the major interruption was a tirade of accusations and filthy name-calling, directed first at Father Virgulak, then at Father Grosso. The entity then made reference to the priests' families and alluded to its interference in their lives:

"Too bad about your brother." "You lied to your sister." "This is going to kill your father." "I'll make your nephew blind."

By two o'clock, Father Virgulak was at the point in the ritual of rebuking the entity and commanding it to leave. This brought on a new wave of violent resistance. Infused with a bolt of strength, David suddenly broke free from constraint and started to run berserk. It took more time to bring the boy under control.

In response to the commands of exorcism, read line by line, there was constant verbal resistance. When shouting and physical struggle didn't work, effusions of spit and phlegm poured out of the boy. Then his whole body was caused to vibrate up and down. This was followed by a choking seizure. David turned blue and stopped breathing. His chest swelled.

By 3:00 A.M., the defiance—both physical and mental—by the entity was undiminished. It was the people who were wearing down.

"Get out of my brother!" Debbie screamed. "Get out! Get out!" She was hysterical and had to be led from the room.

Father Virgulak persevered. "Who are you? What is the name by which you are called? Reveal your name!" he commanded.

In reply came defiance and verbal garbage.

"By the authority of God, I command you to say who you are, or say the name of Jesus!"

"*No . . . never!*"

The command was repeated four times. Finally the entity broke.

"*My name . . . is . . . Legion . . . We . . . are many. . . .*"

Did this mean there was one—or many? Before the night was over, both Ed Warren and those in Brookfield learned the answer.

Unknown to those surrounding David that night, another crucial part of the exorcism was taking place twenty-five miles away.

The scene was Ed Warren's study. There, alone, between 2:00 and 3:00 A.M., Ed Warren received a visitation of a very high and profound order; he was confronted by the origin of all the trouble. That night, Ed Warren *saw* the devil that possessed David.

The entity was not there by chance: it had been summoned! By Ed Warren. Deliberately, for the purpose of "binding" the beast.

"When Paul Bartz called and reported that David came under possession just after midnight," states Ed Warren, "I knew what had to be done. The beast entity had to be bound. It had to be *made* to obey. Binding is an essential part of the Roman exorcism, in which the entity is not only expelled from the body, but it is commanded—or bound—by the law of God not to seize a particular human being again. A diabolical entity that is not bound by the exorcist is capable of possessing again—and again. Therefore, binding, in effect, is the killing stroke.

"But no binding procedure was going to take place in Brookfield. It couldn't—it hadn't been authorized. The Roman ritual hadn't been authorized, because of Church politics and bureaucratic insensitivity. My intention was therefore to summon the lead entity to me—in the name of God, of course—and bind it to a mystical law it must obey: 'Thou shalt not possess another creature of God as thy own.' If I could bind the lead entity, as I'd done before in other cases, then the priests could exorcize the remaining spirits in the boy. This would effect a full exorcism and permanently free David from bondage. What I didn't count on was the complexity of the spirit that arrived."

Having commanded the entity to appear, using the steps prescribed in an arcane religious manual, Ed Warren felt the room grow exceptionally cold. Since the beast needed heat to manifest itself, Ed knew it was coming.

The stench of putred flesh filled the air. Then Ed

heard distant screechings. As a deathlike stillness permeated the room, a sense of immense danger and jeopardy filled Ed's heart. Then, suddenly, the thing was there.

What came through was an entity so horrendous, so radically different, so consummately powerful, that it cannot be accurately described. What confronted Ed Warren, from twenty feet away, was not even remotely human.

It was a pulsing, tar-black mass, seven feet tall. Its body was glossy and throbbing. But it was to its head that Ed's eyes were drawn.

Its head was twice the size of a man's, and it too was pulsating and black. It did not have one face. It had many!

There were features that might be classified as eyes, and a nose, and a mouth, but nothing stayed in one place. Every few seconds the face changed; and with each change came an incredible new grotesquerie. Some were mutilated. Some showed as human abominations with hairy boils on the skin, swollen eyes, and torn mouths. Others were unworldly monsters with jagged horns protruding from the cheekbones, the forehead, or the temples. Still others looked distinctly animalistic, with large red reptilian eyes the size of baseballs, and the snout of a lizard. What Ed Warren saw resided far beyond the confines of human experience.

"What I saw," explained Ed, "was the full show of faces that David vividly described all summer. His descriptions were accurate. What he didn't know—because to him each image was projected as a separate entity— was that all forty-three were *one*! And every face had a meaning.

"Every travail David and his family experienced came through in the faces: hate, rage, violence, profanity, gluttony, deception, malice, pride, betrayal, blasphemy, death. Each face was severe—shocking, in fact; but as a whole the entity was overwhelming. It could not be dealt with. Binding was impossible. If I had started, it would have killed me. I stepped back from the thing, which was growing larger as I watched, and released it from the command by which I had summoned it. The entity lingered a few moments, then was gone."

In Brookfield, the task of exorcizing this pernicious, multifaceted, diabolical power from David continued meanwhile, without let-up.

"*Satan, take my life! Take my soul! Take me, Satan! Take my soul!*" The pleas were bellowed out in David's voice, or what sounded like him, in resistance to the increasing commands of exorcism.

Emotions were frantic and nerves were raw.

"Mommy, mommy, please, this is David Michael Glatzel. Please make them stop. I can't make it anymore. Tell them to stop. Please, mommy. Hurry. I need a rest. I'm going to die! I'm going to dieeeeeee. . . ."

Again and again the possessing entity brought David to the point of death, trying to blackmail the priests to stop. Many times the tactic almost worked. This was the situation at 4:30 A.M.

"It's killing my baby! It's killing him!" Judy shrieked, finally breaking down.

"*I'll kill him! I'll kill him! I swear, I'll kill him.*" the diabolical thing declared.

On the floor, David lay stone-cold still.

It appeared as though David had actually experienced a heart attack. The pulse and heartbeat were nil. The boy's skin grew white. His body lay motionless, seemingly depleted of life. By the time a full minute had passed, those in the room could not help but take it for real.

At this uniquely wrong point in time, Arne Johnson reaffirmed the tragic mistake he had made before. All night long he'd been holding David's arms and legs; all night he had fought and overpowered the physical strength of the entity. Now David lay limp, white, and apparently dying. Desperate to save David's life, Arne declared, "Let David live! Take me on! *Come into me!*"

Deep, coarse laughter promptly erupted from David's inert body. *"Suckers! Fools!"*

The action caused Lorraine to burst into tears. "I immediately sensed that Arne Johnson had made a very grave mistake; that somehow he would be made to pay for his challenge. Not even a priest would say such a thing. Arne made the statements selflessly, to help David, at the expense of himself. But he was ignorant of the responsibility he was taking on by making such an invitation. He didn't know that this thing—instead of releasing David—could actually possess them *both*. Each of them in their own way. Father Virgulak had to stop, take Arne aside, and sternly warn him: 'Don't ever say that again!' "

By 5:30 A.M., the possessing entity had indulged in every possible ploy, both physical and intellectual, to disrupt and stop the exorcism. Finally, there came a sign of weakening. Resistance slackened. All night long the entity had fought to conquer and overwhelm those in the room. Ultimately, it failed. It failed to break free and impose its will on all those present; it failed to carry out its threats to kill David; and, most significant of all, it failed to stop the exorcism. It had lost every battle. It could do no more. Physical strength was beginning to diminish in the boy. The replies switched to rationalizations instead of defiance.

"I don't need this fat little body to be here! I have been here before, and I will be here later!"

The time had come.

That which possessed David Glatzel could either remain, and be forced to capitulate to the commands of the exorcist, or it could stop the possession and withdraw. The latter possibility posed the largest danger, for if the entity withdrew without concession, control would be lost. Possession might end, but the case would not.

"In the name of Jesus Christ, I command you to leave this boy's body! Begone! Leave him in peace!"

"His soul is mine."

"His soul is his own. It is of God, not of you," Father Virgulak told it. "Obey the commands of God set down to you! Leave this Vessel of the Lord! Begone from this Lamb's body! Depart this seat of God's Creation and return to whence you came!"

In response came a sudden, gasping heave. David's body, restrained both at hands and feet, arched violently into a bow, then froze in that posture. His breathing stopped. Anxious moments passed. But again, it was only another tactic of interruption.

Holy water was administered, and David's body crashed to the floor. However, an animal wailing came out of the boy from the "burns" imposed by the holy water. It was a ruse for sympathy, but it did not work.

"The Lord commands you! His son commands you! His Holy Spirit commands you! Cease your audacity! Cease your wickedness! Flee from this boy! Your strengths are weak against the might of God! Cede the wrongness of your act! Release your ignoble grasp! Surrender to God what is His! Depart and begone from this child forever more! This I command you, in the name of Jesus Christ!"

"His soul belongs to me!"

"Depart from him!"

"Never!"

227

"Depart from him!"

"*No!*"

"Depart from him!"

"*His soul . . . is mine!*"

"Depart from him!"

"Stop it! Shut up! Shut up!"

"Depart from him! Cease and depart from him!"

"*I will kill you for this!*"

"There will be no killing. Depart from him!"

"*I will kill him!*"

"You will kill no one. Depart from him!"

"*I will possess another!*"

"You will possess no one else. Depart from him!"

"*You have no authority!*"

"Depart from him!"

"*I don't obey you!*"

"God the Father commands you! God the Son commands you! God the Holy Ghost commands you! *Begone* from this boy!"

Instead of rebuttal, there was silence. The entity that possessed David had fought ruthlessly to the end, and was now weakened, depleted, and beaten. But until now, it had made no concessions.

By slow, barely perceptible steps, that boy which the family knew as David began to come back to them in the early morning light.

The grimace that distorted the child's face slackened and relaxed. The unnatural strength in his arms and legs flooded away.

Immediately, Father Virgulak addressed the entity, its menacing trace still evident in David's eyes.

"Who are you? By the authority of the Blessed Trinity, I command you to give out your name, or show a sign of departure!"

Only tortured sighs issued from David in response.

Father Virgulak crouched down beside David where he lay on the floor and said, "Through the power of Christ, I command you: tell us your name, or give the sign of your departure!"

This time, an answer was given. The reply came not in a bellow or a shout, but in a voice that was distant and barely audible. It was only four words, but those four words said it all:

"*I . . . am . . . the . . . devil.*"

The time was 6:15 A.M., September 9, 1980. That was the last exorcism.

The possession of David Glatzel was over.

Chapter XXI

Chief of Police John Anderson,
Brookfield Police Department:

"We received a call from Ed and Lorraine Warren of
Monroe in October 1980. They said they were involved
with a family that resided here in Brookfield: that the
involvement was pertaining to a demonic possession of
someone in the family, and there was the potential for
great danger."

CBS Morning News
March 20, 1981.

    Given the grave nature of the situation, and its
potential to cause alarm in a small community, all as-
pects of the Brookfield Possession Case were kept strictly
confidential. The Glatzels and the Warrens remained
silent on the matter. Similarly, church officials decreed

that details of the possession had the "status of the confessional" and therefore was privileged information and could not be made public. The whole affair was shrouded in total secrecy. Indeed, it is a case no one would ever have known about, had a gruesome tragedy not occurred six months later as the final culmination of events.

The tragedy came in the form of a murder. A stabbing. It took place in Brookfield on February 16, 1981.

The individual accused of the crime was Arne Cheyenne Johnson. Brookfield police arrested him at 7:25 P.M. on that date, an hour after the fatal incident occurred. He was found walking along a road, reportedly in a "daze." Half an hour later, Arne was charged with murder.

The police asserted that eighteen-year-old Arne Johnson willfully killed a man with a long-bladed buck knife that they found at the so-called crime scene. Those present at the time of the killing, however, witnessed something entirely different.

On an ordinary February day, without warning, the portentous threats and predictions made by the beast the preceding summer came true.

How did this come to pass? What was the *link* between the summer possession case and the stabbing that took place in February?

The spirit had supposedly been exorcized in September. What happened during the intervening months that caused this disaster to occur?

The truth is that what began on July 2, 1980, did not end on September 9. There was one more act that had to be played out in this mystical drama: the death scene.

The combined effect of all the religious procedures

conducted during the summer—the blessings, the High Mass, the concerted attempts at exorcism—functioned to stop the possession of David, the outrageous physical attacks on his body, and the intense phenomena in the Glatzel home.

However, despite all that had been done, the spirit was not conclusively exorcized!

Only the priests left. The spirit did not.

As Ed Warren explains, "Although the various exorcism procedures ultimately stopped the entity from possessing David, the spirit itself was not exorcized—at least not in the classical way the word is understood. The problem had to do with procedure.

"What was required all along was for a trained exorcist to be assigned to the case by diocesan officials and given the authority to conduct major exorcism—the Rituale Romanum. It was the only solution: there never was any other solution. What was possessing David had to be fully exorcized and then bound by command not to possess the child again and to leave the family for good.

"Instead, diocesan officials, accountable only to themselves, stood aloof. The devil in Connecticut? In our diocese? No one must know! We'll take care of it our own way. *Their* way was to do too little too late. After September second, when the need for correct procedure was critical, the diocese *still* refused to grant authority either for major exorcism or for an exorcist—an older man, pious, with the gift of discernment, who has commanded the devil before—to be brought in to perform the task. Because of pride or politics or lack of interest, this enormous job was left in the hands of the four young priests in the field. And they got hurt because of it. Had someone in the chancery gotten off their throne and observed the great evil that was taking place in

Brookfield, some positive move might have resulted. But what took place instead were two otherwise dedicated attempts at lesser exorcism. The result of these 'deliverance' procedures was to stop the entity from possessing David. But the thing was not bound and expelled. It remained free to possess another. Disaster was not stopped—it was only deferred.

"Further exorcism was required. But, unbelievably, the chancery *closed the book* on the case at that point. Father Virgulak was taken off the case in late September and sent to Rome, as Father DiGiovanni had been. The local priests were instructed to return to their regular duties. The policy diocesan officials adopted was that if the entity wasn't possessing David, then their job was done. And they stuck with that position. Instead of cooperation came hostility; instead of peace came tragedy. A metaphysical time bomb was left ticking."

Ed Warren's statements were confirmed by the Glatzel family. Judy summed it up in one terse comment: "The church abandoned us."

"A week after the last exorcism took place in this house," Judy said, "a monk arrived here late at night in a limousine. He and his chauffeur came in and stayed an hour and a half. Father Virgulak was present that night too. This monk was pompous and rude. Ed Warren called him an 'official Church debunker.' He declared that we were all crazy and that David wasn't possessed; his chauffeur blamed Debbie for all the trouble. He said the only devils that exist are Rockefeller and the crooks in Washington. He said that exorcism wasn't needed in this case, and then he left. He insulted me, my family, and Father Virgulak. From that point on, we never got help from the diocese again. They turned their back on us and there wasn't anything we could do about it. The beast was given a free hand to act, and it did."

Incomprehensible as it may seem, this is the situation that prevailed after the summer of 1980. The result was a downslide into catastrophe.

"In September," says Debbie Glatzel, "the thing possessed David a few more times just to show us it was here. But toward the end of the month and into October, the figure directed its attention to little Carl and turned him into a violent madman. We were living in hell again. None of us had any way of stopping this thing; the priests had been scattered, and as a consequence we all became its victims. Carl, for example, pulled a loaded shotgun on me and threatened to rearrange my face; he sent Alan to the hospital with stab wounds in his stomach from an iron rake; and my mother was black and blue from trying to break up these battles. Most of the time, Carl's excessive anger was directed against Arne, my mother, and me. Arne became his favorite target: he destroyed every shred of clothing Arne had; he cut up all his music tapes; he destroyed cartons of cigarettes as soon as they were brought home; he ruined Arne's new work boots by filling them with axle grease the day he got them. Carl, or rather the beast working through him, did everything he could to break Arne down, but Arne never broke. He shouldered it all. It took the beast to step in finally and ruin him."

By mid-October, havoc in the family became so violent and threatening that Brookfield police were called to the Glatzels' home once, sometimes twice, a week. It was only the Warrens' intercession that saved young Carl from being taken away by the police to a juvenile detention center.

"The police didn't know why they were perpetually responding to disturbance calls at the Glatzel property, and they were beginning to lose patience," said Lorraine Warren. "In October, it became necessary to inform them, in as discreet a manner as possible, that a theological case was in progress with the Glatzel family, one that had required Church involvement since July. It was explained that the source of the trouble was not the people, but rather an unexorcized force that was oppressing them. The potential for violence in the case had become a reality, the police were told, and even the possibility of death could not be ruled out. They were requested to keep the family under surveillance but not to arrest anyone unless it was absolutely necessary. Fortunately, the police agreed, and oppression of young Carl died down naturally in November."

On October 14, 1980, Mary Johnson fled the rental house in Newtown with Arne's young sisters. Day by day, all summer and into the fall, little incidents kept building until the girls were so frightened that they refused to go into the house without their mother. Not only did Mary Johnson and the girls see things, hear things, and feel things, but their personalities were changed by the house. They fought fiercely among themselves. Nothing went right. By October, living in the house had also broken them financially. As a result, they were forced to return to Bridgeport, where they live today.

In late November, Arne and Debbie also made a move. Debbie's job at the kennels in Newtown had been phased out in September, but the owner had recommended her to Alan Bono, the new manager of the Brookfield Kennels on Route 7, not far from the Glatzels' home. Mr. Bono telephoned Debbie in late October and offered her a job and a free apartment if she came to work for him. The apartment was in the four-unit block he managed on the property along with the kennels. Debbie took the job—and the apartment.

"Mr. Alan Bono was a very nice man," said Debbie. "He was thirty-nine years old, and had spent the last seventeen years in Australia. His stories were fascinating. Alan had been back in America for about a year, and was managing the property for his brother-in-law. But he didn't know anything about the kennel work; in fact, he hated animals. He begged me to take the job, but at first I told him no, because the kennel runs were filthy and the animals weren't being treated properly. But then he called me back again, and this time offered the apartment. Given the constant war going on with Carl, Jr., I took the job so that Arne and I could get out of the house and start our life together."

So, in late November, Arne, Debbie, and Jason moved to the Route 7 apartment. Arne continued to work full time as a tree surgeon, while Debbie managed the kennels for Alan Bono. With two incomes and no rent to pay, they could save their money, and they were planning to get married in the spring.

But there would be no spring. There would be no marriage. With the move to the new apartment, the stage was now set for disaster. Arne was now installed at the scene of the crime. Alan Bono would be the victim.

In the Glatzel house, activity had calmed down by December. Yet, the beast remained present, in its array of forty-three forms. They knew it was there because it still talked to David, telling him future events, which he passed on to the family. By the onset of winter, the entity was simply a lurking presence.

"What is the beast doing today, David?" Judy would ask.

"He's just waiting, he says," David would reply.

"Waiting for what?" she'd ask.

"He won't tell me," David always answered.

The fact that the entity remained is the telling link between the summer possesson case and the February murder. That which remained had the potential to possess again. And it did. The victim, though, was not David. Nor was it young Carl. The victim was Arne Johnson.

During the summer, Arne had experienced two flagrant possession seizures, the second of which was a humiliating scene in church. On November 4, Arne came under possession a third time.

Arne and Debbie had gone to the rental house in Newtown to check on Mrs. Johnson and the girls, hopefully to repair relations. However, when they got to the house they discovered it was vacant, as she and the girls had fled two weeks earlier. Both Arne and Debbie were glad to see she was gone.

Debbie refused to stay in the house and immediately went outside, where she ran into the landlord's daughter and a friend. A minute later, when Arne walked out of the house, he was possessed. It happened suddenly and unexpectedly the minute he shut the door and put his feet on the front step.

"First, Arne's body trembled violently all over," said Debbie. "Then the whole appearance of his face changed into the same hating sneer that we saw in David all summer. What stood there was not Arne. What stood there was the beast, again, like the master of the house. I almost fainted. It reminded me of all the hell and torment I thought I'd suppressed in my mind. The whole thing lasted less than a minute, but it proved this spirit hadn't left at all, and that it could possess any of us if it wanted to."

It was two months before Arne was possessed a fourth time, in the middle of January. This time Debbie was the only witness. The entity possessed Arne as fully and completely as it had the other three times. As with the previous incidents, there was no talking or communication. That which seized Arne was preoccupied with rage. For the long five minutes that the possession lasted, it virtually ignored Debbie, but angrily punched a hole through a thick wooden chest before withdrawing. "Not even a karate expert could do what he did," noted Debbie, "and the next morning there wasn't even a mark on Arne's hand."

But it was the final two possessions of Arne that led to catastrophe. They took place within ten minutes of each other. Both were fierce attempts at murder. The sixth and last episode of possession resulted in death.

There was no intent or premeditation on Arne Johnson's part to harm anyone: his body was simply seized and used as an instrument to kill. The victim was his friend.

Why the murder occurred precisely on February 16 was not known at the time. But the date was not random: a death was *bound* to occur on that day. The victim was irrelevant, for what was sought by the possessing entity was a human soul. In fact, the intended victim was Debbie Glatzel; but Alan Bono was killed instead.

The reason why the entity chose to work through Arne Johnson was the culminating iniquity. The burden of murder was imposed on him in *direct retribution* for his challenges to the beast at the time it possessed David Glatzel.

In the end, what took place was not just a murder; it was a diabolical execution.

The night before the killing occurred, Arne and Debbie drove to Bridgeport and picked up Wanda,

Janice, and little Mary—Arne's sisters. It was a Sunday night. The next day, George Washington's birthday, was a holiday in Connecticut, and the girls had no school, so they were going to stay overnight with Arne and Debbie. Relations between Arne, Debbie, and the Johnsons had promptly returned to normal when Mary moved out of the rental house.

On Monday, February 16, 1981, Arne Johnson got up at seven o'clock, as usual. He had to be at work by eight. However, for the first time in a long while, he felt ill. He had a throbbing headache, an upset stomach, and chest congestion. He simply couldn't function, and at 7:15 A.M. he called in sick. Debbie gave him two aspirin and an antibiotic*, and he returned to bed. With the chatter and commotion caused by his little sisters, however, Arne couldn't sleep, and he got up for the day shortly after ten. He felt considerably better at that point, but he certainly wasn't well.

Meanwhile, the kennels were open for business that day, and Debbie had a number of grooming assignments and the girls were eager to watch. Debbie introduced the three to Alan Bono, who later invited the entire group, including Arne, out to lunch.

"Alan wasn't married and ate in restaurants almost all the time," Debbie remembers. "He liked to take people out and buy them lunch just to have company. He was lonely. And melancholy, too—he talked about death every day. Arne and I made friends with him just so that he would have friends. But he was a very heavy drinker—an alcoholic. His drinking impaired any ability he might have had to run the kennels, which he hated. The animals were competely ignored. Expensive boarded

---

*Tetracycline, inaccurately identified later by authorities as Mitown.

pets got no food, or water, even no heat. Some died. By eleven o'clock the morning of the murder, Alan was already half-crocked on white wine.

"At lunchtime, Alan took us out to a nearby restaurant, where we all had hamburgers and Coke. Except Alan, who put away a couple of carafes of wine. Alan insisted that we drink wine with him. Arne didn't want to, but we each drank about a glassful. Alan kept topping them up until we let the wineglasses sit full.

"After lunch, we stopped at a pet-supply store and got shampoo and other supplies for the dogs I had to groom that afternoon. When we were there, it was odd, but a big parrot climbed onto Arne's shoulder and sat there all the time we were in the place. It wouldn't get off and pecked at people who came too near him. On the way back, we made a stop at a liquor store, so Alan could buy a big bottle of red wine to work on before dinner.

"When we returned, Arne went up to the apartment for a short nap, I brought the girls to the grooming parlor, and Alan went to work on the wine in the downstairs office.

"It was when we came back to the kennels after lunch that I began to think something was wrong—that something tragic was going to happen."

By 4:00 P.M. that sense of impending tragedy was equally as strong in Judy Glatzel. She began calling the kennels every half-hour, demanding that Debbie and Arne get away from the kennels and return to the Glatzels' house immediately. Debbie sensed what her mother was talking about, and promised to bring Arne and the girls over to the house for dinner at six.

By five that afternoon, Arne was up and feeling better. It had turned into a fine day. Arne joined Alan Bono in the ground-floor kennel office, and was asked if he could fix the speaker wiring in the man's stereo.

Arne set about the task, while Debbie and the girls were grooming in the back.

The poodle was finished and the grooming parlor was cleaned up by 5:30 P.M., when Judy called again. The instructions were straightforward: *Get the hell home!*

"I told her that something was terribly, terribly wrong," Judy recalled. "I knew there was going to be a tragedy, and if we were together, maybe it could be prevented."

But by now Alan Bono was fully inebriated (at the time of death, his alcohol intake registered three times the legal limit at 3.3 on a 1.0 scale), and insisted that they stay and have dinner with him. Debbie resisted, but he created such an obnoxious scene that she capitulated and finally ordered three pizzas.

Shortly before six, Debbie and the three girls went out to pick up the pizzas. Arne, meanwhile, went up to the apartment to check on George, their sheepdog, and to change out of his work boots and into shoes. Curiously, the shoes that Arne put on belonged to David!

It was six o'clock when Debbie and Arne's sisters returned with the unwanted pizzas. They found Arne in the kennel office with Alan Bono, who was still drinking wine. The stereo had been fixed and he seemed pleased.

"I suggested that we have the pizzas up in Alan's apartment," Debbie recalled. "I'd seen it before, and I knew Alan was going to get drunker and fall asleep, and I wanted him to pass out in his apartment, not ours. So I went upstairs and set out the pizzas on his kitchen table, and called everybody, when I was ready. Alan came up last. He brought his wine with him. He also turned the stereo up real loud. It wasn't very pleasant."

Alan Bono, was so drunk that he could barely walk. And he was distinctly not interested in eating. As soon as the others sat down, Alan turned on the television set, even though the stereo was blaring rock music down-stairs. But the television wouldn't work, and Alan began shaking the set and yelling at it.

Debbie told him to settle down, but Alan was oblivious. He began to bang on the wall so violently with his fist that he put a hole in the plasterboard.

Although no one at the table had taken more than one bite of pizza, Arne and Debbie stood up and told the girls that they were to leave immediately.

"Neither Arne nor I wanted the girls to be in the presence of this drunken, violent man," said Debbie, "and we both felt it would be best if we got in the car and went directly to my parents' house. We were certainly not going to stay in the middle of that ugly spectacle."

Arne led the way down the stairs, with Debbie right behind him. At the bottom of the stairs was the door to the kennel office; Arne darted in to turn off the blaring stereo. When Arne emerged from the office, Debbie was holding open the front door. But the girls did not follow. Upstairs, Alan Bono was blocking their way. It was at this moment that the fifth possession of Arne occurred.

"Arne walked past me as I held open the door for the girls, and then he stopped about two feet away," Debbie recalled. "I had just yelled for the girls to come downstairs. Then I turned to get Arne's reaction. When I saw him I shouted, 'Oh no!' It wasn't Arne standing there! The beast was in him! The eyes, the mouth, everything was changed. The next thing I heard was a terrible loud growl come out of Arne. Seconds later I was down."

The entity in Arne Johnson immediately attacked Debbie physically. Within seconds she was on the ground in the doorway, being kicked violently in the stomach, chest, and head. Something was trying to kill her fast, with overpowering force.

"I yelled out, *Jesus, please, have mercy on me!*" said Debbie. "I was desperate. I was being killed. I couldn't defend myself. All I could think was to call on God to stop this thing before I was stomped to death."

This maniacal scene was interrupted by fifteen-year-old Wanda, who by now had come halfway downstairs, moving from one insane situation to another.

"I screamed, 'Arne, Arne, stop it!' Wanda recalled. "But it wasn't Arne, because the teeth were all bared and the eyes were crazy when it looked at me. He looked like the Incredible Hulk. It was awful."

Debbie, meanwhile, took advantage of the distraction and scrambled to her feet. Arne's composure and appearance had immediately returned to normal upon being startled by Wanda. He asked Debbie, who stood crying on the lawn, "What's the matter, sweetheart?"

Janice then came down the steps, followed by little Mary. Directly behind Mary was Alan Bono, who cut in front of the child at the bottom of the stairs and blocked her way.

Wanda recalled, "Mr. Bono was in a rage because we were leaving, and he stood in front of Mary yelling, 'Get back here! You ain't going! Nobody's leaving!' He gave out these orders all drunk, and little Mary started screaming for help."

Meanwhile, Mary, age nine, maneuvered herself in front of Alan Bono, and was about to break into a run when the man grabbed her firmly by the arm. His grasp was so strong that Mary began screaming with pain as well as fright.

"'Come on, Alan, everything's cool,' Arne said," Debbie related. "But Bono wouldn't let go."

In addition to being in pain, the child was also

excessively scared. She yanked and pulled to get free from the man, but to no avail. Her fear, it developed, was for good reason.

Attempts to talk Mary free proved unsuccessful. (From the legal point of view, *forceful restraint of a minor* is a felonious act, and Alan Bono was thus initiating the crime.)

"Let her go!" Debbie told Bono. However, he held on to the girl, declaring that they should all go back upstairs and stay with him.

At this point Arne walked over to Bono. Instead of using force, Arne put his hand on the man's shoulder and said; "Come on, Alan. Let her go. Everything's fine."

But Bono wouldn't let go. He just got angrier. And the child kept screaming from pain and terror.

"*Dammit, Alan, let her go!*" Debbie told the man, and then yanked him by the hair. Distracted, Alan Bono released his grasp, and little Mary ran straight to the car.

"Jannie and Mary were both frightened and crying," said Debbie, "and I told them to get down in the back of the car and not come out." The girls complied to the letter.

Unfortunately, the ugly spectacle did not stop with the release of little Mary. Instead, with his two hands now free, Bono, drunk and angry, attempted to start a fight with Arne.

It was at this point that the sixth and last possession occurred. It proved to be fatal.

The awesome drama that began on July 2, 1980, was about to culminate in tragedy on the front lawn of the Brookfield Kennels, shortly after 6:00 P.M. on February 16, 1981. What took place was the fulfillment of the terrible prediction made the summer before.

On the front lawn of the kennels, in full view of passing traffic, Alan Bono began taunting Arne to fight. When he grabbed Arne, a tussle ensued. To protect himself, Arne grabbed Bono's wrists. Soon their hands and fingers were interlocked in brute struggle, their arms above their heads. The supposedly limp, intoxicated man put up an extremely powerful fight against Arne.

Wanda and Debbie sought to break up the altercation by trying to pull them apart. Debbie courageously wedged herself *between* the two men, while Wanda grabbed Arne around the waist and tried to yank him backward.

"I couldn't budge him," Wanda recalled. "He was immovable. I pulled Arne back with all my might, but he was like a statue."

A few seconds later Debbie extricated herself from the struggle. She was terrified. She saw that both men, hands clenched above their heads, were staring hypnotically at each other. *And Arne was under possession!* His face bore the disfiguring grimace of the beast!

"There were *two* voices coming out of Arne," says Debbie.

"That's true," Wanda confirmed. "One was a screeching voice, the other was a heavy animal growl."

But then suddenly the awful spectacle stopped as quickly as it had started. Or so it seemed. Both men dropped their arms, and Arne began to back away. His eyes were ablaze and his face was distorted.

Debbie sought to approach Arne as he was backing off, but she was immediately repelled with a fierce gaze and vicious, throaty snarling.

Alan Bono, meanwhile, stood in place, smacking his fist in his palm, saying, "Come on! I'll fight you! I'll fight you!"

At that, Arne, still under possession, stopped backing away. A bestial roar, almost in triumph, then issued from Arne's body.

A second later, Alan Bono fell to the ground—face forward. He did not make a sound. He did not clutch for his body. He simply went down.

Arne then backed away completely and disappeared behind the kennels. Debbie and Wanda screamed frantically for help, as they ran to where Bono lay on the ground. They thought he had fainted from drunkenness, or had a heart attack.

"But when I turned Alan on his back," states Debbie, "I saw a slight trace of blood. I pulled up his shirt, and I screamed. He had two stab wounds in him!"

As Alan Bono keeled over and hit the ground, both Janice and Mary were on the floor in the backseat of the car. They saw nothing. However, while Arne was withdrawing from the death scene, a dramatic message was being related to his sister Mary, only. The message was spoken in a man's voice. It said to her:

This is in punishment for Arne's challenges to me. If he challenges me ever again, I will kill him! *I have killed before! And I will kill again!*

Neither Debbie Glatzel nor Wanda Johnson saw a stabbing. Indeed, both insist they never once saw a knife during the whole horrible episode. However, as soon as Wanda and Debbie began screaming for help, Janice and Mary got out of the car and ran to where Bono lay gasping for life on the ground.

It was at that time that a knife was first seen.

"About ten feet away from Mr. Bono I saw Arne's knife lying open on the ground," little Mary remembered. (A wooden-handled folding woodsman's knife, with a five-inch blade. The last time it had been seen was on the table in the kennel office, where Arne had been using it to strip speaker wire.) "The knife had blood all over the blade. I didn't touch the blade, I was afraid to: it was *glowing!*"

Debbie Glatzel, attending Alan Bono, yelled desperately for help. But no one responded; not even people in the nearby apartments, some of whom actually shut their windows.

Frantic and confused, Debbie ran into the kennel office and called her mother. "Help! Please! We're at the kennels. There's been a stabbing here! Arne was possessed! He didn't do it! Please, please, get over here!"

In the background, Debbie heard David screaming and crying.

He knew.

"The beast did it!" David reported. "No one saw it. He just killed with a knife. He went into Arne *and* Alan Bono. All the helpers are there laughing. Arne didn't do it! He didn't do it! The beast stabbed Alan five times with a knife!"

It was true.

When paramedics arrived, Alan Bono was on his back, dying from two stab wounds—one of which had penetrated his heart. Strangely, the first two adults who observed Bono's wounds upon arriving at the scene saw only two stab marks. Minutes later, though, when paramedics went to work on Bono, there were unquestionably four discernible stab wounds to the chest and body.

Cardiopulmonary resuscitation techniques failed to revive the dying man at the scene, and he was rushed by ambulance to the hospital, five miles away.

Alan Bono was pronounced dead in the emergency room of Danbury Hospital at 7:39 P.M.

248

The cause of death? Stabbing.

Number of wounds? Four deep-track stab wounds to the chest and abdomen; one nonlethal stab wound to the victim's shoulder. *Five* wounds in all.

Chapter XXII

Arne Cheyenne Johnson was arrested an hour after the killing. An all-points-bulletin had been put out on him. Ironically, it was not the police who apprehended Arne; but the ambulance driver who'd just brought Alan Bono to Danbury Hospital. The ambulance driver, returning to the Brookfield fire station, had heard the description broadcast on the police radio, and spotted Arne as he walked confused and alone down Silvermine Road, not far from the Glatzels' house.

Arne put up no resistance. Indeed, he was oblivious to the terrible death that had occurred. Near hysteria and still suffering the lingering effects of possession, Arne's only words to the ambulance driver were: *"Please help me!"*

Arne was detained until a police cruiser picked him up five minutes later. He was then handcuffed and taken to the police station. The time was 7:30 P.M.

At 7:40, a call came in to the police station

from Danbury Hospital. The message: "Alan Bono is dead."

Arne Johnson was charged with murder.

Curiously, Arne's response to this charge was to fall asleep! He was reportedly "incoherent and babbling" before that time.

"When I woke up, I didn't know where I was," Arne said. "My whole body was numb. I had no strength at all. I could hardly move my eyeballs."

Arne Johnson's recollections of the night of February 16 stopped abruptly at 6:00 P.M., with the advent of the fifth possession episode, and he did not recover his faculties until he woke at 8:00 P.M., in lock-up at the Brookfield police station, at which time the effects of possession had passed.

Given Arne's previous incoherence, the police read the charge of murder to him a second time. This time Arne Johnson responded with incredulity:

"I wouldn't kill anyone. I *didn't* kill anyone. You have the wrong person. Alan Bono was my friend. I couldn't have killed him."

But no one was listening. Arne Johnson had fallen into the hands of men who would never hear his plea. The police had been called to the Glatzels' almost weekly since the fall, and every trip was a dry run. Now, however, they had Arne Johnson in the station, and under arrest for murder. The police were not about to let him go. They contended that Arne had stabbed Alan Bono to death, using his own knife, which they had found folded up, twenty-five feet from where the victim lay dying. Arne's sisters and fiancé were identified as being present at the time of the killing.

Still, Arne denied committing the crime. He had no recollection of any murder, and consequently he gave absolutely no confession to the police. They would have to prove the crime against him.

As a result, the most critical statements to emerge the night of February 16 were those taken from Arne's sisters and Debbie Glatzel. All four young women described the same events surrounding the tragedy. Debbie and Wanda, the only two eyewitnesses to the death, denied that Arne committed the murder. "Alan Bono just went down," they insisted. How the wounds arrived they could not say.

But in the statements taken from Janice and Mary—who were hiding in the car and *never saw* the fatal event—the police composed incriminating language that linked Arne directly to the stabbing.

Although murder is a capital offense, no lawyer was present at the time Debbie, Wanda, Janice, and Mary gave their statements to the police. The statements were not written by the principals themselves, but *by* the police—and then by only *one* police officer. No second officer was present as an official corroborating witness, nor were tape-recordings made. Most importantly, pertinent corrections were not made to the witnesses' statements, although corrections were demanded by the girls at that time.

The atmosphere in the police station was one of confusion, grief, and high emotions: not the conditions under which to determine the truth. In addition, Mary Johnson had an acute attack of colitis and could not oversee the interrogation of her daughters. In the end, little Mary was made to sign her name to an official statement she could not read or comprehend. And Janice signed her statement believing the policeman would keep his word and take out the references he wrote into the copy claiming she saw Arne stab Alan Bono with a knife. Lastly, once the statements were taken, there was never any countersignature in the specific box provided on the form by a second officer, let alone the chief of police, to verify the authenticity of what had been written.

This was the scene at the Brookfield police station the night of the killing. With the girls' attention fixed on Arne and the appalling possession scene they'd just been through, little attention was given to the official statements taken under conditions that Debbie described as "duress." Yet, those dubious statements would later function prominently in the state's case against Arne.

Despite the fact that Arne Johnson gave no confession and in fact professed no recollection of the crime, and despite the denials of his guilt by those present at the kennels that night, the police took the position that it was nothing more than a simple murder case.

Although the police had been notified as recently as October 1980 that the Glatzel family was involved in a complex theological case that was motivating violence, no consideration was given to that fact when the killing occurred. Rather, by the time the story was given to the press, what emerged was an explanation for a crime that was at variance with what the principals claimed they saw.

Suddenly Arne became the drunken party, who was a "street kid from Bridgeport who knew how to handle a knife." The police charged that on the night in question, Arne had an altercation with Alan Bono—a passive, innocent merchant. The altercation turned violent, whereupon Arne brutally stabbed Bono to death, using his tree-surgeon's knife. Moreoever, during the week, the police ascribed a motive to the crime: Arne was a jealous suitor who killed Alan Bono as the result of a so-called lover's quarrel over Debbie.

For those who were present at the death scene,

this last indignity, this supposed explanation for the death, was, as Debbie puts it, "an utter fabrication that had no relation to reality."

On the contrary, the group declared, "He didn't do it!"

But no one cared.

Arne Johnson was arraigned that week in Danbury Superior Court on the charge of murder, and bail was set at $125,000.00—one of the highest ever levied in the state of Connecticut. Neither the Glatzels nor the Johnsons could obtain such an exorbitant sum. Accordingly, Arne Cheyenne Johnson was remanded to the Bridgeport Correctional Center—barely five blocks from where his mother now lived. The epic had come full circle.

In response to this cruel swirl of tragedy and contradiction, the Glatzels and the Johnsons reasoned that exposing the truth—the *real* truth—was the only way that Arne could be proved innocent. They all believed the truth would set him free. For although those present at the scene of the crime did see death, they also saw possession. But, most critical of all, those who witnessed the killing insisted that they did not see Arne commit the crime of which he was accused. Although the truth they sought to tell was an unconventional one, without legal precedent, it was the only truth they had.

But it was not the Brookfield Possession Case that made headlines two days after the killing. What brought the press running was that a nineteen-year-old male, charged with felony murder, was going to enter the unprecedented plea of "Not guilty by virtue of possession." The plea was promptly misunderstood as a ridiculous copout by another criminal, a new twist on "the devil made me do it."

The bad press and publicity didn't matter to Arne.

What mattered were the contestable statements taken by the police on the night of the killing. Those statements became the foundation for the state's case against him, and were used on March 19, 1981, when an eighteen-member grand jury in Danbury formally indicted Arne Johnson for the stabbing death of Alan Bono.

Janice Johnson said: "I kept telling them [the judge and the jury foreman] that I didn't say those things. I told them again and again that they were the cop's words, not mine. I told them I asked the cop to cross things out that night, but he didn't. He left in what I didn't want to be there. They wouldn't let me say what I wanted to say in the jury room. I wanted to tell them the truth. But I couldn't. They just told me to read the paper I signed [the statement] and not to add anything else. They made my sister Mary lie too!"

Still, the indictment was handed down and the trial date was set for October 1981.

That spring, thousands of letters flowed into Brookfield from around the country and around the world. Pseudo-experts, schooled in matters occult, offered to testify against Arne—and even David—all claiming they had the real answer. One claimed he could "prove" diabolical possession was hysteria (i.e., split personality). Another claimed that the root of the problem was "schizophrenia." A Hollywood magician wrote that the case was a farce and the cause was "mental." When the television series "Quincy" ran a program on the Tourette syndrome or cursing sickness, hundreds of letters poured in diagnosing David not as being possessed but as a victim of the syndrome. ("David was diagnosed for this and other diseases by a psychiatrist during the fall of 1980 and the results were negative," Judy Glatzel stated.) By the time all the letters had arrived, David and Arne were declared as suffering everything from character disorder to neurosis, psychosis, and schizophrenia—and a host of other pathological disorders, including compulsive lying. Anything but the real cause.

One of the vicious consequences of the February killing was that help for both David and Arne through the Diocese of Bridgeport was entirely eliminated. Seeking support from the Church to substantiate the claim of possession, Arne and the Glatzels were "abandoned a second time," according to Judy.

"I'd go to the rectory and they wouldn't even answer the door. I was reduced to stealing my own Communion wafer; I'd save it, bring it home, and give it to David in the hope God would help him."

Rather than supporting the family when they needed it most, diocesan officials released statements to the press that there "was no exorcism" (technically true), and that there were "two separate cases"—Arne's and David's (also true, but one had spawned the other). Church involvement only extended to David Glatzel, diocesan officials claimed, not to Arne Johnson (technically untrue). The rope was cut. Arne, now 19, was truly on his own.

"By the spring of 1981," notes Ed Warren, "the entity had possessed two people and killed another. In fact, the night of the killing, the beast entity replayed the entire stabbing scene to David, who then related the specific details to the rest of the family. The thing had brazenly shown itself to be the author of the crime. Obviously, further exorcism was imperative, so that another tragedy wouldn't occur. What did chancery officials do to solve this looming problem? They transferred Father Dennis and Father Grosso out of Brookfield; in their place they substituted two new priests to flak for the diocese; and they referred all our calls—regardless of urgency—to a lawyer!"

Consequently Arne Johnson was left to sit alone and afraid in the Bridgeport jail. And though he had reason to be bitter, Arne nonetheless remained the same simple and unaffected person that he was all along. This is typified in a letter that he wrote to David on May 12, 1981.

Cell #A10-8A

Hi David,

How are you doing? I'm glad to here from you and I miss you to. I hope everything is going alright for you. I may not be there to help you when you need it. But I pray very hard for you.

I hope thing's are going good for you at school. Do you think you will be down to see me? I hope so. It will be good to see and hear from you again. This way I know your okay.

I pray to get out of here soon. And as soon as I do get out I will be up to see you. I worry alot about you, So keep reading the Bible and pray hard. Because I don't want anything to happen to you, like it did me. And don't forget God is with you at all times.

Tell the rest of the family that I miss them and that I'm all right. So David you take care of your self. And write again soon.

With Loving Paryer's,

Love,
Chey

Given this desperate situation in the summer of 1981, the Warrens found it necessary to go out of the country to seek help for David, Arne, and the Glatzel family. They found it in the traditional Catholic Church in Canada. There, not only was David later exorcized of the entity, but that summer the cause of the whole catastrophic situation was revealed.

"In July 1981, Lorraine and I turned to Quebec to put an end to the matter once and for all," Ed Warren explained. "Quebec is a sort of spiritual powerhouse and many of our most difficult cases are resolved there. In America, once the possession case became publicly known, help was totally impossible for the Glatzels. The Catholic Church in America was far more concerned with bad publicity than its responsibility to aid a child in distress. In Canada it was a different story; the Church there is more traditional and was ready to help.

"Through our connections in Canada, we were put in touch with a man who could exorcize David. He was a gifted priest, in his fifties, assigned to a small church outside Quebec City. Father Deschamps, who administered a busy, suburban parish, was endowed with special wisdom, as we found out. We met with him on July twenty-third, along with a second priest and a Canadian bishop, and discussed the Brookfield case for over four hours.

"Although you couldn't tell it by his outward appearance and manner, he was an exorcist, and a true exorcist has what is called the power of discernment. That means—without being told—he already knows hidden or secret knowledge of a mystical nature. Although Father Deschamps never set eyes on the Glatzels, or even heard their names before, he told us what had happened. For over a year we'd tried to find out the origin of the possession; in five minutes he told us the answer.

"The family had been cursed, he told us. A *death* curse, in fact, had been put on the Glatzels. More specifically, the curse had been levied on David and Carl, Jr. The profane act took place approximately a year before the murder, and it happened in upstate New York. The Glatzel family, he said, considered the people who cursed them to be friends—their *best* friends. However, these people were satanists, and in order to derive benefit from a high devil, they purposefully bound the two innocent boys to a curse—or a pledge of the soul. Activation of this devil entity was made on the day that a member of the Glatzel household—Debbie—was drawn by ordinary circumstances into a diabolically haunted house (July 2, 1980). Everything, Father Deschamps said, unfolded from there."

But what was Arne Johnson's connection to this whole sordid ordeal?

"Father Deschamps explained that when Arne challenged the devil in David," said Lorraine Warren, "he may have saved the child's life, but at the same time the burden of death fell on him. Technically, Arne should have been killed, but the fate of death actually could have befallen any human soul—including us. In this case, the unfortunate victim was Mr. Bono, who was struck at a vulnerable moment. Mr. Bono, Father Deschamps said with total conviction, is with the Lord now. He was killed, through a violation of God's law, by the devil!"

When the Warrens returned to Connecticut, they met with the Glatzels immediately. They said nothing about what the priest in Quebec had told them. They simply asked the family the pivotal questions.

Yes, the Glatzels told Ed and Lorraine Warren,

they had friends in upstate New York. Yes, the Glatzels also said, these people had been considered among their *best* friends, until recently. "But," Carl Glatzel stated, "we no longer deal with them. Somehow trouble always erupted in our home after these visits."

Who were these people, the Warrens asked, and how had the Glatzels met them?

Carl Glatzel told the Warrens the name of the people in question, explaining that they'd met on a snowmobile outing in 1976. "On winter weekends," said Carl, "I'd bring Judy and the boys to a snowmobile lodge in Old Forge, New York. That's where we met these people, and we became friends. Once a year we'd meet for a weekend and snowmobile together—family to family. They were a married couple, our age, with two kids; we were married with three boys. We got along well. But after we separated, there'd always be trouble. David lost his spleen one year; Carl, Jr., tried to kill David with a rope the next; and in 1979—the last year we met—Judy and I each collapsed with sciatica. That was the year we went to their house."

"While you were in their home," Lorraine asked, "did you see anything that might be interpreted as occult implements?"

"Yes," Judy replied after thinking, "there were chalices, candles, daggers, and a skull in the house! Their dog had messed all over the rugs, too, and they hadn't cleaned it up. Their bedroom had blood-red walls and black velvet furnishings. They had a sort of altar set up in there, with black candles and a chalice and a curved dagger all laid out."

"When did you take this trip?" Lorraine asked.

Judy left the room and got a calendar for the year. When she returned, she told the Warrens that they'd taken the trip in February.

"On what date?" Lorraine asked.

Judy's answer: February *16*,—the precise anniversary date of the Brookfield murder!

A total metaphysical connection! The Warrens then explained the connection between the murder and the family's snowmobile friends in upstate New York. Carl and Judy were stunned at the malicious wickedness brought upon them by people who feigned friendship. Oppression, possession, exorcism, physical injury, and even the tragic death of an innocent man had transpired without the family ever once understanding the cause and origin of their travail. Now the answer was known. But there was nothing the Glatzels could do. The worst had already happened. They could only try to free David from bondage and attempt to keep Arne from being sent to prison.

This information, revealed during the summer of 1981, finally led to a resolution of David Glatzel's case. In the fall, correspondence and pertinent information flowed north, including a twelve-page request for exorcism. In October, after much consideration, the request was granted. Major exorcism, however, was not called for at this stage, as David was no longer possessed. Instead, what took place in a small stone church just outside Quebec City, on the snowy morning of November 7, 1981, was a "charismatic deliverance."

There was great dignity to the event. The technique employed was the classical form of exorcism known as "the laying on of the hands," in which the afflicting force is expelled *through* the body of the exorcist. The entire procedure took less than thirty minutes. When it was over, the author of all the evil experienced by the family was finally identified. Its name was a shock to all.

Two priests were required to effect the deed. One

served as exorcist, the other as religious medium. All members of the Glatzel family were present. David, dressed in a shirt and tie like his brothers, sat in a straight-backed chair in front of the family.

Father Deschamps, the exorcist, placed his hands on David's shoulders. The other priest, Father McEwen, working as medium, took David's hands into his own.

Then Father Deschamps began:

"In the name of the Father, the Son, and the Holy Spirit. Amen.

"Almighty God, we beseech your indulgence.

"St. Michael, protect us.

"By the authority of Our Lord, Jesus Christ, the Redeemer, the Protector of mankind from the wickedness and snares of the devil, I command you, in His name, to leave the body and soul of this child, and return to your place in the pit of Darkness."

Immediately there was a reply from the possessing entity. Aghast, the family heard the voice of the beast— but, incredibly, this time it came not through David but through Father McEwen.

It demanded: *"Let go of the boy!"* Father Deschamps did not reply. *"Let go of him! Get away!"*

"You are the Defeated One!" the exorcist said sternly. "In the name of the Lord Jesus Christ, I command you to give us your name and depart!"

"You are just a man!"

"I speak as one, with the authority of the God of Heaven and Earth. In his name, I command you to leave! God commands you to leave. His Son . . ."

"Stop it! Stop it!"

Debbie felt a searing pain at the base of her neck. Alan turned cold. Carl, Jr., leaned forward in rapt attention, staring at his brother, while Father Deschamps, holding on firmly to David's shoulders, began to shudder.

Still, he continued to command the spirit out of the boy: "Reveal yourself and leave!"

"Nooo!"

"In the name of Jesus, leave!"

Suddenly a loud crash of glass sounded next to Carl Glatzel, followed by hard poundings on the wall directly behind a statue of the Blessed Virgin.

"Say your name and leave!" Father Deschamps ordered in a powerful voice, now undergoing an intense physical ordeal.

"Nooo."

"Heed Christ and begone!"

Papers on a nearby table began to fly around, as though a gust of wind had blown through the church. Then more vicious poundings walloped the wall by the statue. Whisperings of a multitude of voices filled the air.

"Name yourself!" the exorcist demanded, his body now shaking frenetically as the possessing spirit entered him. "In the name of Christ: capitulate! Obey the commands of God! *Name yourself now!*"

The atmosphere was one of pure crisis. Something was bound to happen. A point of such danger had been reached that there would either be resolve, or pandemonium would suddenly explode in the room.

Miraculously, moments later, the entity capitulated. At that, the voice of the beast spoke one final time. It gave the mandatory sign of departure by revealing the horredous name by which it was known. It was the devil second only to Satan. Through the mouth of the medium it declared to all:

"I . . . am . . . BEELZEBUB!"

Silence followed. The exorcist, soaked with perspiration, withdrew his hands from David's shoulders. The child was clear. So was Father Deschamps.

The next words came from the mouth of Father McEwen. Astoundingly, in David's voice, he announced: "Mommy. Mommy. I'm free! I'm free! I'm free!"

Out of the gray Quebec sky fell a wet, white snow. For David, for the entire Glatzel family, the havoc was over. Relief and intense appreciation was felt by all for the resolve attained that day. Yet, deep down, there was no true joy in their hearts. Although David may have been free from bondage, Arne was not. The legacy of the beast remained. Arne's case had come to trial.

Arne Johnson's trial began on October 28, 1981. In May, Arne had been given the option to plead guilty to a lesser charge of manslaughter. But Arne Johnson's reply to this plea-bargaining effort by the state was that he did not kill anyone, so he refused to plead guilty. Arne asserted that the state of Connecticut had accused him of murder, and consequently they would have to prove it was so.

Set in this conviction, Arne sweated it out in an inner-city jail during the hot summer months and into the fall, anxious to prove his innocence, and certain that the truth would set him free. He remained firm in his belief that trials were designed to expose the truth and absolve the innocent of wrongdoing.

The proceedings were held in Danbury Superior Court, a large domed structure at the far end of the city's Main Street. As would become the daily pattern, Arne arrived at the courthouse that morning in a white sheriff's van with bars on the windows. The vehicle looked like it belonged to the dog pound. Local and national media reporters and photographers gathered around the truck as Arne Johnson was led into the building. He was wearing a suit and tie Debbie had bought him.

Although the proceedings were scheduled to start at 10:00 A.M., the gavel didn't come down until 2 P.M. Thirty-five minutes into the start of the trial, the devastating blow arrived.

Arne's attorney—who took the case at no charge after seeing the murder written up in newspapers—asked a prospective juror if he believed in God. The juror answer yes. Then the attorney, testing the waters, asked, "How about the other way—do you believe in the devil, too?"

The gavel came down and the proceedings were stopped.

The presiding judge, Robert Callahan, asked Arne's attorney if his question bore a relation to a defense of possession.

The attorney answered yes.

Obviously prepared for this eventuality, the judge immediately issued a premeditated and absolute ruling that he would not permit a possession defense to be advanced in his courtroom. Period. He stated that Arne's attorney had not filed the proper procedural form* for the defense of a crime involving mental irregularities; and that there was no legal precedent in American law for pursuing the "unscientific" defense of possession.

Thunderstruck, Arne's attorney objected strenuously to the sudden and "prejudiced" ruling. He cited his client's right to a fair trial; the right of the accused to present any defense that proves innocence; the inapplicability of insanity in the case; and finally that the evidence of possession was critical in Arne's case be-

---

*Ref: Rule #758, Connecticut Practice Book.

cause it affected his client's *intention* to commit a crime—the very basis of the murder law.

The judge listened obligingly, then rejected all the defense attorney's points. He contended that possession couldn't be proved; that it didn't affect intent; that demonology was not a science but a "hobby"; and, most incredible of all, that the notion of diabolical possession was "irrelevant" to the crime of which Arne was charged.

Unbelievably, even before the trial began, the judge dismissed the very essence of Arne Johnson's defense.

For Arne, it was an outrage. In effect, the state of Connecticut had simultaneously charged him with the crime of murder and denied him his Constitutional right to defend himself. Because the underlying facts made the public uncomfortable, they were disallowed, leaving Arne with no other defense, save to lie. Arne Johnson was standing trial for his life, but anything he might have said in his own behalf was barred from the courtroom the very first day.

Thus began the trial of Arne Cheyenne Johnson. The media reporters and photographers left. "If it ain't sensational," one paper openly declared, "we won't print it." Had he only known!

The judge's ruling not only muzzled Arne's defense, it also threw open the door for the state to make virtually any case it wanted against him. And it did.

The state prosecutor took full advantage of the pejorative ruling to press a straightforward murder case against Arne. Amazingly, the state's case amounted to a parroting of the Brookfield police department's initial rendition of the crime.

Accordingly, the prosecution asserted that Arne Johnson stabbed Alan Bono to death in a drunken brawl. The real devil was alcohol, said the prosecution, and under its influence, Arne lost control of himself and killed Alan Bono, a tweedy, pipe-smoking chap who was the victim of an unconscionable rage.

To drive home this claim, during the first week of the trial, the state brought in a parade of expert witnesses—medical examiners, pathologists, toxicologists, and police.

However, none of the experts could directly link Arne to the crime! Blood found on the knife was type O—the same blood type as Alan Bono's—but the blood could not be positively identified as the exact blood of the victim. Furthermore, although Arne was supposed to be in immediate proximity to his victim, no blood was found on Arne's shoes or clothes. The large folding knife that Arne used in tree work had no fingerprints on it; consequently, it couldn't be positively identified as being *the* murder weapon. Lastly, no positive connection could be made between the victim's wounds and the knife that was exhibited in court; any similar knife could have done it. The only thing the expert witnesses managed to prove was that Alan Bono was dead.

Failing to establish a true physical link, the state instead turned to Arne's sisters during the second week of the trial. Debbie Glatzel, who should have been the prime witness, was never even called to testify. During the grand jury proceedings she had described the death of Alan Bono the way she really saw it, and the prosecution therefore wanted no part of her.

What developed was an ugly scene where sisters were pitted against their brother and *made* to testify against him, vis-à-vis the highly contestable statements taken at the police station the night of the killing.

But the girls would not comply.

They had come to tell the truth, the whole truth, and nothing but the truth; the state, however, *insisted* they ratify the fiction of stabbing and drunkenness. The girls tried to say that Arne didn't do it. The state said they were committing perjury by not affirming the statements prepared by the police the night of February 16.

Caught in the terrible crossfire, the girls cried on the witness stand. But they would not lie and betray their brother. Not one of the girls said she saw Arne stab Alan Bono with a knife. Instead, they recanted the original statements attributed to them the night of February 16, and were then declared "hostile witnesses."

After the state had made its case, Arne's attorney, in a last-minute gesture, asserted a secondary defense. He contended that on the night of the killing, Arne had come to the aid of his younger sister, who was being forcibly detained by a violent, intoxicated man who was *already* engaged in felonious behavior. The defense attorney contended that Arne had come to "the self-defense of another," and in that circumstance, force was required to save his sister from further harm. Had Alan Bono acted like a gentleman on the night in question, the lawyer contended, Arne wouldn't be in court today.

In the end, the state took two weeks to make its case; the defense, two days. The state depicted Arne as drunk the night of the crime; his sisters were depicted as liars. Yet, a man was dead, and Arne's knife was found at the scene. Who else could have done it? Who else allegedly had a violent altercation with the victim just before the death occurred?

The state closed by asking questions instead of by supplying answers. It never explained where the knife came from; it never explained why there was a discrepancy in the number of reported stab wounds; it never solved the enigmatic question of how the wounds arrived; and it never proved intent. The jury was simply asked to bridge the gap of appearance and reality with facts that were never provided. The state, failing to prove that Arne committed the crime, instead pointed to the mass of circumstantial evidence and official testimony, and asked the jury in conclusion to *infer* that Arne did it.

The trial ended on Friday, November 20, 1981. The jury never got to hear how the murder really happened from those who witnessed the event. Nor did the jury ever learn about the Brookfield Possession Case, and how it was the true origin of the crime. It had been fed truly one-sided information, then given the task of rendering a verdict based on a false scenario. A pretense of justice had been played out, but it all seemed so senseless and unreal. For Arne, the Glatzels, and the Johnsons, the court proceedings were but an extension of the iniquity that began a year and a half earlier, on July 2, 1980.

Now, mindful of the beast's prediction that "Arne would be put in jail without a trial," the family wondered if the case would ever end.

At 3:00 P.M., Friday, November 20, the judge charged the jury with the responsibility of coming to a decision based on any one of three verdicts: *murder* (the commission of an act with the intent to kill); *manslaughter* (the commission of an act with the intent to injure); or *not guilty*. Whatever the decision, the jury's verdict had to be unanimous.

At 3:30, the jury left the courtroom and began its deliberations. The longer they remained out, the greater the possibility that Arne would be found not guilty. The first day, the jury remained sequestered until 9:45 P.M. but failed to reach a verdict. Word leaked out that the jury was "confused"—they had a mass of information that seemingly proved nothing. At 10:00 P.M. the judge sent the jury home for the weekend and instructed them to return on Monday morning.

Remarkably, despite all the sorrows and hardships, the Glatzels and the Johnsons remained hopeful.

On Monday morning, November 23, the jury returned and continued their deliberations. They remained sequestered all day. They were indeed confused. Question after question was issued from the locked room. By 5:00 P.M. no verdict had been reached. Again the jury was instructed to return in the morning.

On Tuesday, November 24, the now beleaguered jury took up its deliberations at 10:00 A.M. Again, questions were passed to the sheriff, who sat outside the locked oak door.

In the hallway, the Glatzels and the Johnsons waited through each painful hour. But they were optimistic. The jury was stuck on the issue of intent, the families were told; and if the jury could not determine intent, then the only verdict they could return was that of not guilty. Debbie Glatzel went out to her car and brought in a clean, pressed suit for Arne. He was coming home!

At 3:45 P.M. a message was handed to the sheriff at the jury-room door. They had come to a decision.

At 4:00 P.M. the panel filed into the jury box, obviously drained by their long, arduous experience. Court was then reconvened. To the surprise of everyone in the gallery, the jury foreman stood up and informed the court that the jury was unable to come to a unanimous decision. The jury panel was totally deadlocked and they were unable to render a verdict.

The judge refused to accept this. He instructed the jury to resume its deliberations and come to a judgment—preferably one that reflected the majority of the panel. He gave them until 6:00 P.M. to find a verdict, or the case would be dismissed.

The jury filed out. Arne Johnson was two precious hours from freedom.

The moments passed with anguishing slowness. Arne's sisters waved to him through the window where he was being held behind bars; Debbie threw kisses; Judy Glatzel prayed; Carl Glatzel paced the hall; Mary Johnson sat staring into the air, a holy card of Padre Pio clenched tightly in her hand.

Then, just before five o'clock, another official note was passed to the sheriff. The jury had reached a decision!

Darkness had fallen outside, as the men and women of the jury filed into the courtroom one last time. Although they'd been deadlocked all day long, and had another hour to go, no one could predict their final judgment. Strangely, the wall lights flickered briefly in the courtroom the moment the panel was seated.

"Have you come to a verdict?" questioned the judge.

"Yes, we have, your honor," the foreman replied.

Arne Johnson was told to rise and face the jury. Clean-shaven, in a tie and sport coat, Arne stood up, oblivious as always to the facts of the crime that he was accused of committing.

"Look the defendant in the eyes," the judge told the foreman of the jury, "and inform him of your verdict."

The foreman stood up and looked at Arne. "The jury," he announced, "finds the defendant *not* guilty of murder!"

An immense sigh swept across the bench where the Johnsons and the Glatzels sat listening.

But behind Arne Johnson, another voice was heard. What it said was directed only to him, and heard only by him. The coarse voice uttered one word. It said, *Beware!*

The foreman of the jury then spoke again:

"To the charge of manslaughter in the first degree, the jury finds the defendant *guilty!*"

Arne's knees buckled. His lawyer had to help him stand. His mother, Debbie, and Judy burst into tears. The worst had happened. The next sound heard was the footsteps of a sheriff who walked up to Arne and snapped chrome handcuffs on his wrists. It was over.

Arne Johnson's life was ruined.

The penalty the judge levied on him, for showing compassion in a closed room during a private tragedy in the summer of 1980, was one entirely without mercy.

He was given the maximum sentence possible.

Arne Johnson was sent to jail until the year 2001.

The devil had won.

> All that is necessary for the triumph
> of evil is that good men do nothing.

> ——Edmund Burke

Epilogue

March 1, 1983

It would be a pleasure to say there have been positive developments in this case, but there is no happy ending to report.

Although the overt phenomena have long since ceased, the beast remains, and exerts its pernicious influence over the lives of everyone involved in the case.

Indeed, the entity has interfered in the lives of people quite independent of the Johnsons and the Glatzels. After Mrs. Johnson vacated the rental house in the fall of 1980, a new family took over the property the following spring. The new tenants experienced a siege of such terror in the home that, as local papers reported, they fled the state in the summer of 1981, vowing never to return.

Another example: A hairdresser in Brookfield commented to a patron that she believed the Glatzels' story and hoped Arne would win his case. At the moment she made that statement, a bolt of lightning struck inside the beauty salon, on a clear day, producing scorch marks and knocking out electricity.

More importantly, the Glatzels' lives have never really returned to normal. Those who levied the original curse on the family cannot be found; and even if they could be found, there is no provision for justice against their heinous crime. However, David is no longer beset with the indignity of possession. Exorcism proved successful in relieving both him and young Carl of direct influence by the beast. But David still receives messages and visitations from the entity. Probably the most poignant incident occurred the night Arne lost his case. On that night, David suddenly woke up in the middle of the morning. Moments later, the beast walked through the bedroom wall, holding Arne's folding knife in front of him. The knife was glowing. The entity stood laughing like a maniac in front of the boy, then faded away.

More recently, David reports, he has twice been confronted by the human spirit of Alan Bono—immaculately dressed, smoking a pipe, and asking if everyone will come over to the kennels and work. "Although the man is unaware of his death," say the Warrens, "his appearance to the child in white indicates he has been successful in his transition to death."

But perhaps the most tragic victim in this case is Arne Johnson. He is going through a living hell, with no hope of relief. The prime years of his life are now being lost inside the maximum security wing of the Somers Prison, in Somers, Connecticut; in payment for a crime he cannot recall and that witnesses say he didn't commit. One would have to go all the way back to the trial of Sacco and Vanzetti to find a similar injustice in New England law.

The beast remains with Arne in prison, as it has done since the very first day. Although it has never possessed Arne again, it plagues him with bizarre, threatening nightmares, and occasionally comes to him in physical form, usually as a black cloud. On the anniversary of Alan Bono's death it stabbed Arne in his cell. Although Arne's lawyer proclaimed his intention to bring the case to appeal, there will be no appeal. His lawyer even lost a bid for a sentence reduction in the spring of 1982. The world has abandoned Arne, and he is now very much alone. Only the Glatzels faithfully visit him on weekends. If this case demonstrates anything, it is the unworkability and indifference of our formal institutions, both civil and religious. Nonetheless, Arne Johnson should be given a new trial, or his term should be commuted lest the immorality stand.

Earlier this year, in 1983, the beast presented itself again—this time to Debbie's young son, Jason. It got to the child while he was in the middle of a raging fever. The thing sat on a throne of bats, spewing fire everywhere. Death was on its mind. It told the boy how it was personally responsible for the torture and killing of thousands of people during World War II. It also had a message. The entity said that because man had failed to point *him* out in Connecticut, what has taken place so far is just the beginning. It would, the entity proclaimed, "kill again!"

ABOUT THE AUTHOR

Dr. Gene Scott is a scholar and lecturer who has made a vital impact on Christendom with his Bible teaching to groups encompassing virtually every religious background.

Dr. Scott has the unique ability to demystify truth in light of the day and hour in which we live.

For a book and tape catalogue on diverse subjects including the Pyramids, Stonehenge, the Lost Tribes, the Stars, Atlantis and Basic Christianity, write: Dolores Press, 389 Church Street, San Francisco, CA 94114.